# The Power of Mental Wealth

## Featuring Leutisha D.W. Galloway

# The Power of Mental Wealth Featuring Leutisha D.W. Galloway

## Success Begins From Within

Leutisha D.W. Galloway

Johnny Wimbrey

Heather Monahan

Les Brown

WIMBREY TRAINING SYSTEMS
SOUTHLAKE, TEXAS

Copyright ©2021 by Wimbrey Training Systems

Published by Wimbrey Training Systems
550 Reserve Street, Suite 190
Southlake, Texas 76092

Printed in the United States of America

All rights reserved. No part of this publication may be reproduced, stored in any retrieval system, or transmitted in any form or by any means, mechanical, photocopying, recording or otherwise, without permission in writing from the publisher, except by a reviewer, who may quote brief passages in a review.

ISBN: 978-1-951502-65-2

# Table of Contents

Chapter 1
1............................................... *The Power of Your Will*
Johnny Wimbrey

Chapter 2
15........................... *Free Yourself: Live Without Comparisons*
Judy Crawford

Chapter 3
25................................................ *Falling Doesn't Count; Getting Back Up Does*
Darren McKevitt

Chapter 4
37..................................... *Finding Your Superpower*
Mont'ique "Honeybee" Moore

Chapter 5
49................................................ *Listen With Confidence*
Heather Monahan

Chapter 6
59......................... *Your Outlook Determines Your Outcome*
Bjorn "Beez" Hendricks

Chapter 7
73.................................. *Success Begins From Within*
Christopher King-Hall

Chapter 8
85........................................ *It's Okay To Ask For Help*
Jayln Nicola

Chapter 9
97............................ *Keep Your Chin Up and Stand Tall*
Dolores C. Macias

| | Chapter 10 |
|---|---|
| 109 | *What Brings You Joy?* |
| | Gabriel Retana |

| | Chapter 11 |
|---|---|
| 121 | *Live Life on Purpose and With Purpose* |
| | Yolanda Jones |

| | Chapter 12 |
|---|---|
| 133 | *What Are You Feeling?* |
| | David Peacock |

| | Chapter 13 |
|---|---|
| 145 | *Reach For the Stars and Be U'Nique* |
| | Antoinette B. Seawood |

| | Chapter 14 |
|---|---|
| 157 | *Your Life is Not Beyond Repair* |
| | Andre Nero |

| | Chapter 15 |
|---|---|
| 169 | *Take Pain By the Hand and Walk Into Greatness* |
| | Elyse Arroyo Peña |

| | Chapter 16 |
|---|---|
| 181 | *Turn Your Pain Into Power* |
| | Gavin Fortuin |

| | Chapter 17 |
|---|---|
| 193 | *Believe In Your Own Success* |
| | Leutisha D.W. Galloway |

| | Chapter 18 |
|---|---|
| 205 | *Understand Your Power and Purpose* |
| | Shirley Lancaster |

| | Chapter 19 |
|---|---|
| 217 | *Rising From the Ashes* |
| | Carolyn M. Johnson |

| | Chapter 20 |
|---|---|
| 229 | *Grow Continuously* |
| | Les Brown |

# Foreword

The world has become a more unpredictable and threatening place over the last year. Our ability to survive and thrive has been tested by tremendous outside forces that aren't in our control. Among the few things we *can* control are our perceptions and our thoughts.

*The Power of Mental Wealth* is a book I'm very proud to publish, especially at this moment in human history. This is a time for us to invest in our minds and not squander our mental resources.

Mental *wealth* is a cutting edge-concept, one you may not have heard much about just yet. The concept of mental wealth is just beginning to gain traction as people start to realize its possibilities and immense value.

So how is it different from mental health? Or mental strength? Is it something you can bring to the bank?

More than twenty immensely talented people share their definitions of this term and their mental gifts with you in *The Power of Mental Wealth*. Their chapters include stories of perseverance, overcoming adversities, building self-confidence, increasing their joy, and training themselves to see the brilliance and success of their futures.

In every single case, they worked hard to perfect themselves and improve their minds. They worked on this intensely, investing a good chunk of their time, for years. They all succeeded, and so can you.

Not one of these authors suggests their gifts were just handed to them. They built their mental wealth the old-fashioned way, and they're sharing their results with you. They share the tools they use, such as listening, using their subconscious or all their senses, and building self-worth. They've learned to believe in themselves, create their own realities, and live life by design.

They have mastered the power of their wills.

I am awed by their potential, and even more, awed by their generosity in sharing what they've learned with you.

You can build your mental wealth through what you learn in this book. As world-famous Les Brown writes in his chapter, *grow continuously*.

Invest in your mind. It's the best investment you can make.

—Johnny Wimbrey

Chapter 1

# The Power of Your Will

Johnny Wimbrey

They say a mind is a terrible thing to waste. I'll take this further: I say it's terrible, even unforgivable if you don't commit yourself to strengthening your mental powers and turning them into your strongest assets.

And, honestly, I'm amazed every day by the potential we all have. We are the only beings with the power of self-will. This means that we all possess the mental capacity to obey or to disobey, to lie or to be honest, to love or to hate, and the mental strength to will ourselves past adverse situations to reach our goals. (Setting those goals is a whole other book; I'll tell you about Building a Millionaire Mindset later in this chapter.

None of us are immune to adversity, none are immune to temptation, and none are immune to life's trials and tribulations. Whether we'd like to admit it or not, we all fall short in life at one point or another. Every human being will experience the good, the bad, and the ugly. That's the reality of life. Some situations may seem very small and trivial to most people, but these trivial situations can and do escalate to very regrettable and drastic situations.

We all have faults.

They say confession is good for the soul, so let me come clean to you:

I have no tolerance for people who are late or situations that waste time. I can't stand to be late, and I hate being unproductive. I cherish time because it's irreplaceable; you can never get it back once it's gone. People who are not time-conscious frustrate me. Actually, they drive me crazy.

> *We can develop the mental wealth to be able to afford our dreams, and the mental strength to keep us on track.*

I wasn't born watching a clock; I programmed myself to be time-conscious a long time ago when I was very young. You may be thinking, What's wrong with this? Valuing time is a strength, an excellent tool for someone with ambition, especially for a leader. I agree in principle—but what's also a strength is being able to control your reactions, your will.

Anything you don't master will master you. My reaction to wasted or lost time is an emotion I can almost always control now, but for a few years, I struggled. When I lost my cool, it wasn't acceptable to me or to anyone who was unfortunate enough to be involved. It's a self-inflicted weakness, and it always embarrassed me. This was a real problem for me and others during my twenties.

The problem originally started when I changed my attitude about time. I didn't have the foresight to imagine having to cope with situations that were out of my control. I didn't realize even capable people (like me, I like to think) can make drastically bad decisions when we're not prepared for an unpredictable change that's completely out of our control.

Then one day I took control of my mind and things changed. It was a beautiful, sunny Texas day, I was driving my BMW roadster down an uncrowded road, cruising along, not too fast, with the convertible top down. Good music was playing on the audio system; I was at peace and in the very best of moods.

When I looked up and realized I'd missed my exit, everything changed in a heartbeat. My smile became a snarl and I could feel my blood pressure soar. My peaceful mood exploded into frustration and anger in a matter of seconds. Missing the exit may sound trivial, but you must understand, by the time I got back on course, I lost time—at least a whole five or ten minutes. I found this totally unacceptable.

As you read this, you're probably laughing at me, but I promise you, I'm not exaggerating my instinctive reaction. What's even more ridiculous is that I'd already been conducting seminars and self-help courses around the country. I'd studied a variety of philosophies, and had participated—as a leader!—in several seminars on self-control. And here I was frustrated and out of control because I had missed my exit.

I got off the highway and detoured through back streets to get back on course. As I drove, I began to think about something I had recently heard. It was still fresh in my mind, and for some reason, it really resonated with me:

If you want to get over a negative situation, begin to find positive things within your negative situation.

I figured, "What the heck? I have nothing else to do; let's see if it works." Though I was awash in my negativity and frustration, I began to look for positive things. At first, I didn't see any, so I began to look for simple things. You could call them simple pleasures.

I remember this next moment so clearly, it could have been yesterday. As I drove up to a red light and stopped, I looked at a car turning toward me from the side street. The driver was smiling, a wide, ecstatic grin. I said to myself, "If I hadn't missed my exit, I would never have seen that great grin."

Instantly, like magic, my frustration vanished. I thought, "Man, this is cool." And when the light turned green, I realized the light wasn't your normal green. The light glowed with a brilliant, rich, fluorescent green. And I thought to myself, "That's the most phenomenal green light I have ever seen. If I hadn't missed my exit, I would never have been able to experience this beautiful green light."

Now I must admit all of this was totally out of character for me, but it worked. I began to feel excited, almost as if I were in a competition to find positive things. It was fun!

I'd made a conscious decision to mentally master my out-of-control, overreacting battle against wasted time. Since that moment with the grin and the green light, I've only blown my top over lost time a couple of times. That doesn't mean I've mellowed to the point it where doesn't bother me. Of course, it does! I just control my thoughts, my willpower, and practice my mental strength.

Every individual has the ability to consciously decide whether to master a situation or to be mastered by it. Every individual also has the ability to decide how long he or she chooses to either master or be mastered by a situation.

There is a time and a season for everything. It is very important that you also understand every season will and must come to an end. As I conduct self-development training and seminars around the world, it amazes me to find only 10 percent of most individuals' mental battles are caused by the situation. 90 percent of their struggles are caused by their inability to move on and simply let go of the problem, the habit, or whatever needs to be in the past. I find it difficult to watch a person wrestle with something that would immediately disappear if they could just simply let it go. It drives me crazy to see an individual be overwhelmed and mastered by a ridiculously simple situation, and I find it hard to be in their presence.

I'm working on my shortcoming of patience in this case, too and I know soon I'll be more accepting of their idiotic reactions. But until I succeed in overcoming my aggravation at their bone-headed obtuseness, there are quite a few wonderful people whom I avoid because they, unfortunately, choose to be mastered by preposterous situations. To me, this is a form of mental bankruptcy.

For instance, how can two otherwise loving individuals be willing to have their marriage come to an end because they can't agree on whether the toilet paper roll should be hung with the paper over or under the roll? How could a person be a loving wife and mother one moment and the next moment be booked for homicide because road rage made her lose her mind?

Okay, I admit I made these up. Toilet paper has probably never been the cause of any divorce (except during the pandemic), and road rage can never be an acceptable alibi for murder.

But let's agree on this concept: Good people make bad decisions when they forfeit the right to master an obstacle or adversity and instead allow it to master them. It's said that you can always measure the character of a person by the size of the obstacle it takes to overcome him.

Good people become murderers every day—and good people are murdered every day—because of individuals who simply are not in control of their emotions. Think about it: How many people do you think are dead or in prison either because of their middle finger or someone else's middle finger? I don't truly know the answer, but isn't it ridiculous to think that a middle finger could cause an individual's rage to escalate to the point of deadly force? How hard would it be for most people to prepare or train themselves never to allow someone else's physical gestures to control them?

These days, different political preferences have caused apparently irreparable rifts in families and between friends. Are people going to avoid their best friend or brother forever because a yard sign, a comment, or a social media post made them blow up? Just because the country is not as bipartisan as it should be is no reason they can't have the generosity, love, and the will to accept different viewpoints. They can summon a smile as they work on negative reactions and keep their blood pressure under control.

What and who push your buttons and have the ability to cause you to lose control and step out of your character? When you hear the words "lose control," it's probably a natural instinct to think of individuals who are literally out of their minds or crazy. We hear these phrases all the time: "He really went off the deep end this time," "She just lost it," or "He just flipped." These are extreme examples, but we lose control every day without having the excuse of real mental illness.

Individuals who are not conscious of the fact that they are capable of losing control will adopt the habit of losing control. And one who adopts the habit of losing control creates the lifestyle of one who's out of control.

On the positive side, control can be regained. If you ever said, "I can't believe I just said that," or "I apologize for snapping like that," you were actively regaining control. You were making a deposit into your mental wealth account, and the next time around, it'll be even easier to recover your equilibrium.

Are you conscious of the moments where you're less in control, and willing to clearly accept and admit that you're being mastered?

I was once told that you should manage your weaknesses and master your strengths. I'm not saying we can ever be successful at mastering all of our emotions and every situation, but I am saying every successful step forward is a step toward being the master rather than being mastered. I believe if you practice mastering the basics—or what some would call the minor things in life—you are actively positioning yourself to avoid potential disasters. You are developing your will.

Is it possible to be in control in a very intense and heated situation? Absolutely! Let me give you an example.

Have you ever seen an NFL highlight special? It's like an R-rated version of a Super Bowl highlight special; there's no editing, and you can clearly hear everything the football players are saying on and off the field. It's mind-boggling to see a 300-pound man tackle another 300-pound man on the field, watch them both crash down onto the ground with one on top of the other, faces distorted with rage, screaming insults and yelling into each other's faces, close enough feel the spit. Then the referee blows his whistle, and bam, it's all over. They help each other up, perhaps even with a friendly pat, and walk back to their huddles as though the tackle never happened.

How can a warrior type of guy, someone who is so revved up with total focus and intense energy, filled with competitive emotions, regain complete emotional, physical, and mental control in a nanosecond, just with a signal?

Do you know what's really crazy? That same football player with the willpower and discipline to walk away from someone who's spitting in his face and screaming insults while slamming him to the ground is the same guy who gets arrested the next week for a bar fight with a drunken football fan who calls him a loser.

Could this be the same person? And by the way, aren't legal penalties for breaking a drunken loudmouth's head more severe than a ten-yard penalty from the NFL?

For years, these players have been mentally conditioned by their coaches; they completely understand that the consequences and penalties coming from uncontrollable behavior on the field are simply not worth the risk. The mental conditioning is at least as important as the physical training. Their results speak for themselves. Many of them just don't carry this discipline out into the rest of their lives. They don't see it as an asset they can use wherever they are—a form of mental wealth.

The questions to ask yourself are these:

Who's coaching you to understand the adversities you will face in the real world?

Who's teaching you how to evaluate the risks?

Who's teaching you how to control your mind and develop your will?

Who are your mentors?

Let me repeat: We are the only creatures with the gift of self-will. This means that we do possess the capacity and the power to control our minds. We can develop the mental wealth to be able to afford our dreams, and the mental strength to keep us on track. We just need to find the coaches and mentors to help us reach our potential.

Our minds are terrible things to waste. Please don't waste yours.

# Author's Notes

My first childhood memory was living with my mother and brothers in a homeless shelter for battered women. As a teenager, I hung out with a tough group of friends and even owned a gun because it was expected of me. My path seemed predetermined—and then suddenly a friend was murdered and I did an about-face, using my self-will for the first time.

I began to build my mental strength and mental wealth, and I changed my life. I got a job, went to college, married my sweetheart, wrote a best-selling book, From the Hood to Doing Good, started my journey to wealth, and began speaking around the world. I coached, mentored, and founded philanthropies. As CEO and President of Wimbrey Training Systems, I oversee and create programs for personal development, wealth and career management, sales training, and speaker instruction.

I've also been a TV and radio host, and the co-author of several additional books, Multiple

Streams of Inspiration, Conversations on Success, Break Through, P.U.S.H. (Push Until Success Happens.

My newest solo book, Building a Millionaire Mindset, is being published at the end of 2020. In it, I focus on entrepreneurial success and lay out a simple "building block" approach to growing your business to the million-dollar level. Each chapter deals with a single task you must complete before you move on to the next one, and I share my insights and give you tools to help you make it happen.

My wife and best friend, Crystal, and I live a busy and fulfilling life in Southlake, Texas with our three wonderful children—our daughter's Psalms and Hannah, and our son, Honor.

## Contact Information

# Johnny D. Wimbrey

Master Motivation/Success Trainer
**Most Requested Topics:**
Motivation/Keynote
Overcoming Adversity
Youth Enrichment
Leadership/Sales
**www.JohnnyWimbrey.com**

 @Wimbrey

 Wimbrey

 Wimbrey

 JohnnyWimbrey

Johnny Wimbrey

Chapter 2

# Free Yourself: Live Without Comparisons

## Judy Crawford

When I was five years old, I suddenly realized my family was poor. My parents were fighting over money because there wasn't enough to pay the bills, and Dad yelled, "We might have to live on the streets!" The terror of actually becoming homeless shook me to my core. That fight was a pivotal moment in my life, and it changed me forever.

Even at my young age, I had already determined I wasn't going to live the way we did when I grew up—I was going to live differently. I accepted the fact that I didn't have control over my situation as a child, but I absolutely *knew* I'd be able to change my life when I became an adult. I was a big dreamer as a child. I was so introverted and shy that all I had were my thoughts and dreams.

I grew up in East Los Angeles, a poor, Hispanic community a few miles from downtown Los Angeles, in the opposite direction from the beaches. Even though I am Mexican, Hispanic, and Native American, my light-colored complexion came from my paternal grandmother, who was Spanish. My light skin kept me from fitting in with the others, so I didn't have friends and I was often the butt of other children's nasty teasing. Children can be so cruel without knowing what they're saying is mean.

> *Comparison is truly the death of joy.*

My family was large—five kids—and I am the youngest. We wore clothes from the Salvation Army or hand-me-downs from our older sisters. Every year my sisters and I each got one new dress for the Christmas holidays. That new dress always felt like a celebration, and I was sure it was the best thing ever. No matter how poor we were, I have to say we were always meticulously clean, with our hair done, clothes immaculate, and everything that was supposed to be white was super white. Each one of us always looked very put together.

But I knew my clothes were not new. To this day, I will not walk into a consignment store no matter how high-end the store is, because I just can't bear the thought of wearing someone else's clothes ever again.

I hated going to school because I never felt welcome. Starting in kindergarten, I ran away from school a lot, always heading straight for our house. The first few months, I ran away almost daily, and I somehow managed to find my way home across streets and through at least a mile of rough neighborhood, sort of like a homing pigeon.

When I showed up at the front door the very first time I ran away from kindergarten, my older sister immediately loaded me into the car, drove me back to my classroom, and handed me over to my teacher. I decided I needed a sneakier strategy, so from then on, each time I left school and made it home, I'd wait outside where my family couldn't see me until I thought it was too late in the day for them to drive me back. I remember plotting out my moves so clearly, even now, decades later.

After a few years, my mom lost all patience with my running away from school. At times, I feared she might go off the deep end if I continued, so I finally stopped leaving class and running home from school. I still hated school, though!

My brother was four years older than I was, and he was also being mistreated at school. The few times he had lunch money, someone would steal whatever he had. They'd threaten to punch or hurt him to make him give up his cash. When I was nine, my parents had enough, finally, and said, "It's time for these kids to go to a school where they're not beaten up and don't want to run away." They made the difficult decision to send my brother and me away to live with our oldest sister, 30 or so miles from home.

I was *so* excited to have this new adventure. Moving into a new house, going to a new school with the hope that finally I could find some friends and be happy at school. Up until this point, I despised everything about school.

The night we moved in with my big sister, I was wound up and couldn't sleep at all. It was a lot to take in. Instead of sleeping in the dining room at my parents' house, I shared a bedroom with my niece, and we had multiple bathrooms to use. It was a whole new world.

This new world wasn't all sunshine and roses, though. My older sister was having an affair with a very well-off married doctor who gave her an unlimited supply of prescription drugs, keeping her pretty high most of the time. The doctor also supported all of us financially, paying for the house, utilities, food, and most of the family's necessities—just about everything except clothes.

I didn't realize until my first day of school that I now lived in a very well-off neighborhood. My circumstances changed from deep poverty to great wealth in an instant, and my life was very, *very* different. I now went to a primarily white school, and even though I was light-skinned, I was asked many times if I was Mexican.

It was a reverse of what happened in my first school in East L.A., where I was often asked if I was white. There I'd always answer, "I'm Spanish, Mexican, and Native American," but the other kids wouldn't believe me.

Asking these questions has never made sense to me and I've never understood why race matters to the people who ask, but it is very obvious this is very important to them. I've never even *thought* to ask anyone about their race or ethnic background. I've always felt it shouldn't matter, that we're all the same—just people.

What overwhelmed me in my new surroundings was the sheer amount of wealth all around me. I was the poor kid in the hand-me-down clothes taking the public bus to school, surrounded by kids with expensive new clothes and riding in the beautiful cars their parents drove. I had never even seen cars like those before!

I realized I was now living at the opposite end of my parents' spectrum. I was surrounded by money. Most of my friends had whatever they wanted because their parents were wealthy.

By the time I reached high school, I had many friends, and they were amazing people. We had a "tribe vibe" going. Though I had a blast with the social part of high school, I still didn't like school itself. My freshman year was a disaster, and I pretty much failed every class, even PE.

My father sat me down and had a talk with me. He told me I had to take school seriously if I wanted to improve my life by going to college and finding a career I loved, one that financially supported me. He finally got through to me, and I decided I was going to do the work and try my best to be a better student. During the next school year, I had much better grades and I was much happier about school.

At this point, I learned all about "comparison," and, oh, my goodness, I suffered because then I couldn't *stop* comparing. I compared my situation, my clothes, my hair, the cars, the houses, myself, my *everything* to everyone else's. I lived this way for years! I was miserable, but I didn't know any better.

In school, I would walk down the hall and say to myself, "She's got great hair and mine is awful," or "Look at her shoes and look at my ugly ones." I compared to the point of sometimes even not wearing shoes to school because I couldn't stop comparing mine to other people's more expensive and better-looking shoes. My logic for going shoeless was simple and hard to argue with: *I can't compare feet because we all have feet!* Inevitably, I would be sent to the office, and they would make me put on my shoes.

I was victimized many times by my own thoughts because I never said nice things to myself. The way I talked to myself was just awful and rude, and I was meaner to myself than anybody else had been or could be.

Things began to change when I took a class in public speaking. For some unknown reason, I allowed myself to become open and vulnerable for my first speech, and I shared how at times I felt defeated by my own thoughts. Not only did I get an A on the speech, but many of the other students also came up to me afterward and told me I helped them to realize they were being their own worst enemy at times.

It was liberating to hear I wasn't the only one having such negative thoughts. I was relieved to learn the private discussions I had in my head were common among people, even the ones I was convinced were full of confidence and had it all together.

At that time, I didn't realize all my experiences would have great meaning when I grew up, and they would impact my life in the business world. Now I've realized I could never have achieved all that I have accomplished if it hadn't been for these painful experiences. When I remember these awkward times in my life, I realize I was not a victim, but a person learning how to adjust and pivot for whatever life throws at me.

Every one of the painful moments has been educational, and I am very grateful to have gone through what I did and come out the other side appreciative rather than bitter. I know I could have very easily gone down the victim path.

As a young adult, I took all of these experiences and applied all of the good I learned about myself and about people. I tried college for one semester, but college just didn't resonate with me at all, and by the time I was 19, I was ready to go out into the real world. Because I could type more than 100 words per minute, my speed and accuracy helped get me in the door of a small law firm where in theory, I was the litigation secretary, but for all practical purposes I was the *everything* girl: answer the phones, type, open mail, make appointments, banking, and make post office runs. I did it all.

I learned everything I could, and after three years, I left for the big leagues—a great job with an exceptionally large law firm in downtown Los Angeles. That's where I met my husband, and life just took off from there. We married, had a daughter a couple of years later, adopted our son soon after that, and off we went.

After we decided to move away from Los Angeles to California's Central Coast, I really hit my stride and started racking up some notable accomplishments, especially in real estate. My career milestones include serving as the president of our town's real estate board, and I led us through the many adjustments we had to make during and after the 2008 market crash. Our town's association stayed financially healthy during my term as president, even in 2009, when we were in the throes of the great recession. I've had great success in almost everything I have done.

As well as working on my professional skills, I invested time, energy, and money into my personal growth. A great therapist/life coach worked with me for the next 10 years, but I didn't stop there. For more than 35 years, I've focused on how to perceive things differently than the way our mind wants us to believe.

I've learned to look at *everything* as a learning experience.

It's incredibly important to me to have a mentor in my life, and my husband has been a great mentor to me. His experience with coaching high school football and mentoring many young men has also been impactful for me. Many of his players come back to either coach alongside him, visit, offer support, or just to say "hi" because he made such a change in their lives. When I see his impact on these young men and its obvious value, it reinforces the importance of mentorship at a young age. Most importantly, I've learned our lives are meant to be learning experiences.

We need to focus on the big picture of what we're learning and doing, and not get caught up in minutiae, negativity, and comparisons.

Comparison is truly the death of joy. Comparing yourself to others will literally kill any joy in you. I learned that lesson late, unfortunately, because I never had a true mentor as a young person. I was an adult before I had a mentor to warn me how destructive what I was doing to myself was and to stop doing it. Once I learned to stop comparing, my life changed, and I found my joy again!

My biggest life lesson was learning to live from a place of *compassionate detachment*. I have compassion for people and situations, but I am detached from the outcome. That is the one thing that has been the most important in my growth.

We can't worry when things go sideways or even just not as we planned. I lived my life with worry for far too long, until finally, I realized worrying is a waste of time and energy. When I understood I don't have any control over the outcome, no matter *how* much I worry, life became so much easier. Accepting that concept has helped me tremendously in life, and especially in business.

I love to help others see that they can have the life they've always wanted and dreamed of by eliminating worry and living their lives free of comparison.

# Author's Notes

My life is going amazingly well. Real estate has been very good to me and I'm transitioning into retirement with a leadership role in my new business venture in the technology field.

More than 20 years ago, my husband, Tom, and I decided the big city life wasn't for us, and we moved to the beautiful Santa Ynez Valley in Santa Barbara County. We love the pace and quality of life here on the Central Coast of California. Our daughter, Kelley, lives in Sweden, and our son, George, his wife, Maudia, and our two grandkids, Beau and Gianna (GG), reside close by.

## Contact Information

    **Email:**        judy@judycrawford.com
    **Website:**    www.judycrawford.com
    **Facebook:**  www.facebook.com/judy.crawford.106/
    **Instagram:**  judymcrawford/

Chapter 3

# Falling Doesn't Count; Getting Back Up Does

### Darren McKevitt

Ireland, my home, is a small island with a lot of heart and potential. I believe the Irish people are evolving more and faster now. We have great men and women who are smashing their self-limitations and personal beliefs and becoming whomever they choose to be.

It took me a while to get to that point, though. At a noticeably young age, I developed a negative mindset. I had no mental wealth or focus and never felt as if I was *enough*. A lot of the bad habits I developed came from my family's beliefs and perceptions and the environment around me. I grew up in a broken home. My father was not around much. Alcohol, drug abuse, and crime were his way of life, so I was raised by my working mother, who struggled to hold down a job and care for me.

It wasn't always bad—there were good, happy times as well. When my father was around, you could see that beneath all the baggage and tough exterior, there was a strong love. But that didn't offset what was happening all around me while I was growing up.

My hometown was flooded with heroin. Every night there was always something chotic happening on the road—if it wasn't car chases or joyriding, it was stabbings and shootings. Mostly, though, it was ego-based arguments over who was better than whom. (Apparently, they thought they had their reputations to uphold.) Growing up, that was my normal, and I had unknowingly become a product of my environment. Now, don't get me wrong—I had a part to play in all of it. I loved the madness! But why did I love it?

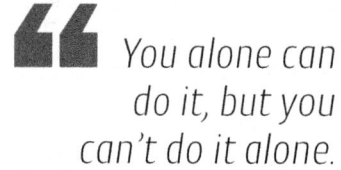
*You alone can do it, but you can't do it alone.*

When I was eight years old, I had my first trouble with the law. I was caught with a sports bag full of sweets, crisps, and cakes taken from a local shop. As you can see, even at that age, I wasn't settling for mediocre. I wanted it all or nothing. My wildness continued as I got older. I started smoking hashish when I was 10, and by 11, I was selling drugs.

By then, I had experienced my family's struggles as we scraped by, my mother working a hard job, five days a week, and having nothing to show for it beyond our living expenses. My mother made sure I was cared for properly and did it well and on her own. Throughout all of it, she stuck to her morals, but I didn't want that for my future. By then, I had witnessed how easy it was to make money in different ways and I saw the lifestyle having money can bring.

I wanted it.

I wanted *all* of it, no matter what the outcome might be.

Growing up, I was a terribly angry child. I had witnessed a lot of violence in my home and community. When I didn't live up to my own personal standards, I would turn it inward and criticize myself in a horribly negative way that in turn left me feeling like an empty shell. My ego was damaged, and I felt worthless, so I countered that feeling by engaging in bad behavior as my escape, which was my way of deflecting pain.

By 15, I had lost a limb while stealing a motorbike. I was always stealing. I had to—I needed the buzz, the excitement of it. Every time my mother and I would go out to shops, I would fill my pockets, and *boom!*—the thrill would hit me.

That is where my self-worth, self-talk, self-belief, self-perception, and self-discipline went out the window along with any bit of backbone I had left. I had no self-discipline whatsoever. I felt very vulnerable—quite different from most people I knew.

After losing a part of my body through my own actions, I was bombarded with horrible thoughts and feelings. My friends and I would joke about it, but subconsciously it was affecting me on a deeper level. I was being hit by the full gambit of disempowering thoughts like *you're not whole, you're weak, you can't do this, you're less than everyone else.*

The thoughts brought on a lot of fear and even more fearful thoughts. It became repetitious and created a cycle of anxiety. In response, I began to take more drugs and commit more crimes. As the years went on, my mind was consumed by negative messages and my world grew worse as negative opportunities would present themselves. There was crime, violence (against me or someone I knew), drugs, parties, and a lot of hate talk against me or someone I knew.

By the time I was 20, I was addicted to pills, cocaine, weed, alcohol, sex, and crime. My diet was terrible—I can't recall a full week of healthy eating. I was always eating takeout food and eating it too quickly and at unreasonable times and in unreasonable amounts. I chose food for the flavor, with no care for nutrition.

At every moment, I was selling drugs and anything else I thought to be profitable, constantly chasing money. The obsession was there, along with the drive and desire, but the more I chased money, the more it ran from me. I had no money management skills whatsoever, no structure, and no self-discipline or self-control. As I turned 21, I got myself into a lot of debt with multiple drug dealers, the police were all over me, and my life seemed to spiral out of control.

I lost everything but still had an unstoppable ambition to do better and get out of my mess. I had a vision in my head of me being wealthy but nothing else beyond that. I signed myself into rehabilitation to get myself together and become a different person. The Christian drug rehabilitation center was my first attempt to do some work on myself. During my three months in rehab, I had a spiritual intervention. It was inexplicable to me at the time, but I knew something had changed within me.

As time went on, I fell back into the trap of drug abuse, negative thinking, and out-of-control behavior. I was not being consistent with my new behaviors and habits. Hospitals, jail, and rehab became my new habits, and I would delude myself into thinking I could have a positive life while behaving and speaking critically of others and most of all, myself.

After doing a lot of reflection while I was in the hospital, I decided to change my life. I was a 28-year-young man and had nothing to show for it. I could see my vision and what I desired moving further and further away. I decided to go ALL in, with no half-measures. I realized that no matter what we do in life, we must give it 100 percent or it won't work. So, I took everything I had learned from over the years and started to apply it.

When you are on a journey to spirituality, to change, to make money, or whatever it is, if the small little daily habits of self-evolution are consistently attained, well, then, our outer world will also change. Think of it like playing snooker. If you are off by a millimeter when hitting the ball, the outcome will be a major change in direction at the end.

While I was in the hospital contemplating life, an opportunity presented itself to change my whole life, and that was to go back into therapy—a therapeutic community, which means therapy 24 hours a day, 7 days a week. At first, I turned my nose up at the opportunity because I already had been through therapy, thank you, and I thought, "I'm not doing *that* again."

After doing more thinking, I realized I had to drop my ego, be humble, and admit defeat once again. I did some research on the facility where the therapy would take place and found it to be the perfect place to heal myself mentally, emotionally, physically, and spiritually.

It turns out I have a knack for psychology, philosophy, and self-development. *I love this.* The fact that you can become the type of person you want to be just by changing your behavior is fascinating. Trying to figure out life is appealing to me. I want to learn more about life; how it works, and how thoughts and behaviors can make our reality. Now my vision has become a lot clearer: I want to give back; I want to help individuals like myself who were stuck in a rut. I want to change their minds!

You must give back whatever you took from life. What that means is whatever you benefited from, whether materials, emotions, or knowledge, you must pay it forward. I wanted freedom. I wanted a good and honest life where I held myself accountable for everything that happened to me during my life, including the bad choices that I chose to make.

Everything you go through in life is for your benefit. When you figure that out, you will master life.

When I got out of rehab, after doing 18 months, I was a new man but I found myself in the same world. I still was in the early stages of recovery, and I started from rock bottom with a fresh mindset. Money was the furthest thing from my mind because I wanted to learn more about *myself*.

Success is about achieving your goals, overcoming addictions and vices, and taking whatever is thrown at you as you keep moving forward.

One of my toughest vices to overcome is that when things get tough, I sulk, I don't get anything done, and I will throw my toys out of my baby carriage, metaphorically speaking. I get angry and revert to what was always comfortable. I'll eat unhealthy food and I do harmful things that stop me from progressing.

Look at it like this: A business takes one to three years of build-up to be successful. Building yourself up from scratch to fully become who you want to be, takes the same amount of time. So why are we so scared to fail along the way?

Most people will not succeed because they don't want to be seen failing, or they are afraid to step out of their comfort zone. But there is a whole other world waiting just outside the window if you allow yourself to see it.

To be successful is to fail multiple times. As Johnny Wimbrey says, just swing the bat; it doesn't matter if you miss, just swing and get going. Let go of perfectionism because it will literally stop you from moving forward.

One year after being out of rehab, I was still very much getting used to what life as a different person is like. At that point, I decided to get going with making my theories into my new reality. I got out the laptop and began to write. As time went on, procrastination began to set in and all these self-limiting thoughts filled my head: *Who am I to think I can do this? Who do I think I am? I will never be able to this?* Fear sat in and blinded me from seeing the way through. I had an *I can't* attitude. The funny thing about all of this is that it's just in my head.

I developed a morning routine—a 4 a.m. wake-up followed by hypnosis, yoga, and meditation, then going straight into a cold shower. The routine was giving me a clearer mind, but not only that, I was handling the problems life was throwing at me without taking them so personally. But again, I wasn't consistent, and I went at it on and off for ages.

Despite my lapses, I really did realize there was absolutely nothing to stop me from achieving the lifestyle I aspired to, no matter what. That obsession was getting stronger. No matter how many times I failed, I always got back up and moved forward, getting further than my last attempt.

Finally, I built a resilient mindset. I looked at every role model out there and adopted their habits. I got rid of everything that wasn't serving me or the lifestyle I wanted to achieve. I became extremely grateful for everything in my life and realized the power of giving back. As time went on, I added more micro-habits and began growing more self-sufficient with a well-developed ***I can!*** mindset.

To build mental wealth, we must first push through our mental challenges and build enough self-confidence to achieve any goal. Yes, it's a struggle to utilize the importance of micro-habits and to put them into daily practice. Yes, we fall, and sometimes we stay down. *I have*—thousands of times. It's a matter of finding the power that's buried deep within and letting that bugger come back stronger than before. When we accomplish anything in life, either small or big, we must congratulate ourselves and pat ourselves on the back.

You alone can do it, but you can't do it alone.

You must become self-aware, and by doing so, look out for the patterns that occur *before* you fall. This can prevent you from staying down when you fall, or even falling at all. The more you bounce back from the shit life can throw at you, the quicker you can get back on track. The most important thing to look at is that we grow and learn from our failures.

A great way to change or reframe a situation from a negative to a positive is by saying *I love it!* and then doing your best to *mean it*. For example, fear would set in whenever I thought of writing. My fear blocked me mentally, but the more I told myself I loved it, the more I was able to break free and actually fall in love with it.

A strong person is held accountable for his actions, not his voice. We need to hold ourselves accountable for every little thing in life, including words, no matter the circumstance. As time goes on, the obstacles that looked big start to become small. Fear does not have a presence anymore and we begin to move forward quickly.

We can adapt to a winner's mindset by broadening our perception of what success is because success means different things to each of us. I believe reinventing ourselves by gaining new skills is the only way to get free from that stuck-in-history version of ourselves we probably imagine. Our brains are like software; if they aren't updated regularly, we become less useful. When we regress in life, we can reverse the direction. No matter what we want to change can be changed, from habits to traits to personality disorders.

We can become anyone we want to be, *but only if we do the work.* Our reality is formed by our perceptions, beliefs, and habits. We cannot fully step into a new world unless every part of us is changed; otherwise, it would be like putting a cassette into a CD player.

Through self-awareness, daily practice of growth challenges, and putting your true self first before anything, our self-esteem—our power—begins to rise.

# Author's Notes

I was born on Halloween, on the southside of Dublin, Ireland, to a family that was quite small, to be honest.

After my early years of crime and addiction, I made the conscious decision to change my life. My rehab was 18 months long, including an extra three months, I believed I needed.

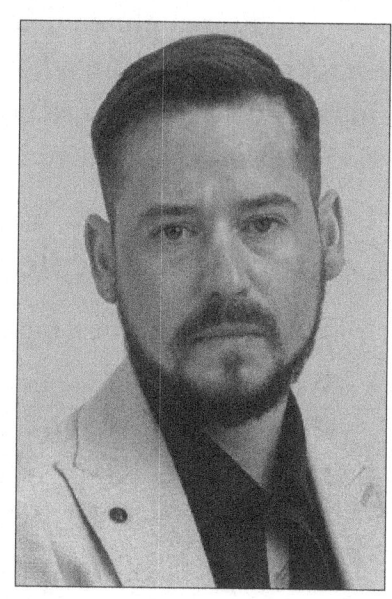

Now that my whole mindset has changed, the opportunities that are presented are good, positive, fun, and safe. Everything I've learned over the years, including the tools I gained in therapy, helps me level up challenges with an I-can attitude, no matter what is thrown my way. I understand the challenges are for my benefit, which enables me to use them to my advantage.

The people in our lives change us and reflect us. This is why I was so honored to be chosen as a co-author by the world's best multi-millionaire coach and best-selling author of *Building a Millionaire Mindset*, Johnny Wimbrey, along with the world's number one motivational speaker Les Brown, and the marketing and woman's empowerment guru, Heather Monahan.

I'm now certified in holistics coaching specializing in hypnotherapy, and help people to start and scale a six- to seven-figure online business. These are things people dream of—and through hard work and sacrificing your old life, such dreams are possible.

So, dream big and go for it without fear.

## Contact Information

**Email:** info@darrenmckevitt.com
**Website:** www.darrenmckevitt.com
**Facebook:** Darren Mckevitt
**Instagram:** @darren.mckevitt
**Twitter:** @THEIRISHALCHEMIST

# Chapter 4

# Finding Your Superpower

## Mont'ique "Honeybee" Moore

Have you discovered your superpower? Do you even know if you have one? Well, if the answer is *no* to either of those questions, allow me to present you with your most important tool for success: *mental wealth*.

When we analyze the more commonly recognized concept of financial wealth, we realize it can only be acquired through mental wealth or just plain luck! Even if you're born into wealth or inherit some form of wealth, it takes a particular mindset to sustain it.

One night after attending a Christian comedy show in a church, the Bishop made his way over to my husband and me. The Bishop approached us with warmth and grace as he extended his hand, and what he said shocked us and has stuck with us to this very day: "I need to shake hands with the money couple."

"Money couple?" My husband, Anthony, and I laughed, looking at each other with puzzled faces because we are just regular working folks making the best of what we have. Anthony said, "Thank you, we appreciate that, but you've got the wrong couple."

The man of God said firmly, "No, I am seeing you just right. I can see wealth all over you, and I know you're the only ones who can get in the way of your own success. God has great things in store for your future if you don't mess it up."

> *There is not one piece of my life—good, bad, or indifferent—that isn't a contributing factor to my success.*

After I heard this, I began to look into wealth a little deeper. What does it really mean to be wealthy? As I searched, I discovered *wealth* doesn't necessarily mean *money*. Wealth is more about knowledge and relationships than the zeros in your bank account. Although it doesn't hurt to have those extra zeros, there is much more to it than that. Yes, while money opens the doors to these rooms and having capital may get you into rooms that you may otherwise not have been invited into, it's the relationship that gets you a seat at the table.

The room may be where the experience happens, but the table is where the magic manifests. So, I asked myself, "Do you want to just be another body in the room, Mont'ique, or do you want to be offered a seat at the table?" I went on a short quest to find the wealth the Bishop said he could see. I say *short* because I didn't have to go far to find it. It was right where I'd never looked for it—inside me and surrounding me!

I found wealth in my good health, my loving and supportive family, and my ability to pay my bills without struggle. My most prevalent wealth is stored-up experience, knowledge, my truth, and my learned behaviors, both good and bad. Once I began to unpack these things from inside myself, it was like finding a hidden treasure box. I realized I had spent so many years chasing my dream to be rich and popular, and the truth is being famous and having money doesn't make you wealthy. In fact, I realized my chase for fame and riches had exhausted me and was detrimental to my purpose, integrity, and character. It's easy to mislead yourself when you haven't identified who you were created to be.

Like many young girls, I embraced a life of rebellion and disrespect. When I was old enough to leave home, I chose the streets rather than dorm life. I was attracted to fast cars, fast cash, fast men, and shopping sprees, and they were attracted to me.

My journey through young adulthood included several dangerous relationships and many hard lessons; I was very lucky to have made it through that stage of my life without losing my daughter and my freedom. My worst experience was dating a drug dealer ten years my senior; he paid my rent and bought me nice things. To protect the guilty, let's call him Frank. Like most immature, inexperienced young girls, I thought we were in love and was sure Frank would marry me someday. I imagined a future for us, one with a lifetime commitment, children, owning a home, and other fairytale flourishes.

Frank and I played house and we played in the streets like we were the best and baddest couple around town. I put up a good front, but the reality was he was mentally, verbally, and physically abusive. Everything he bought for me was like a loan, not a gift, in his mind. The moment Frank wanted to control me; he took those gifts back.

Once I was going on a trip with friends that he didn't want me to make, and I noticed the expensive Coach handbags I had in almost every pastel color were all missing. So were the matching belts and accessories. I asked Frank, "Where are my Coach purses?"

"Those are *my* bags and you aren't going nowhere with *my* stuff," he sneered. This ignited an argument that led to a fistfight. I left for my trip scratched, bruised, and with my hair messed up and half pulled out. You would think I wouldn't go back to him, but I did.

I went back to him because I still didn't know who I was without him. I had no real understanding of my self-worth, and I certainly didn't know I had been born with a superpower I still hadn't used. Though I was created to be more than someone's arm candy or punching bag, I didn't fully recognize it, nor did I understand how cool I was all by myself. I was a daughter of a Father in Heaven who said he has plans to prosper me, not harm me.

At that point, I was more concerned about keeping up with the lifestyle Frank provided me, as wicked as it was, and avoiding any embarrassment. I just didn't know any better at the time. Here is where I need to pause and say, "Thank you, Lord, for keeping your hand on my life when I didn't deserve it."

So, I chose to continue living in a stifling environment of manipulation and control, that was as unhealthy for my daughter as it was for me. On the surface, I moved past all the hurtful things Frank did and said, but deep inside I couldn't forget them. At least all of his hurtful words eventually helped catapult me into realizing my superpowers.

The abuse went on for at least another year before the events that led to my awakening. One day I played hooky from work to hang out with Frank. We dropped my daughter off at daycare and got something to eat. As we drove down the street, we were pulled over by several undercover police vehicles. They had their guns drawn on us and were in full-bore SWAT mode as they arrested us. Turns out, they had been watching Frank for months and today was the day they decided to pick him up. My God, how I wished I hadn't called in sick that day.

The police put us both in the back of the same police car. I felt confident everything would be okay for me; I knew that I'd never done anything illegal or sold drugs, and Frank never made any transactions in my presence. So, I wasn't overly concerned about what they would do to me until I discovered that the man I was convinced loved me, the man who was fully aware of my little girl was waiting for me to pick her up from school—*that* man—expected me to hide his drugs from the police on my body.

I don't understand why I was so surprised when this man who had abused me privately countless times in the past put me in that position. I should have expected

It. This is where I must pause and say one more time, "Thank you, Lord, for keeping your hand on my life."

Now to protect the innocent from any presumption of guilt, I will just say that what should have been a felony conviction for me ended up being a six-week program followed by a sealed record. Frank did his time, and I will just leave it there.

When I came home from the arrest, my house had been torn inside out by a police raid. The warrant was for finding drugs; thankfully, Frank had never brought that poison into my apartment.

Finally, I was wide awake. I could see the forest through the trees and realized I'd been blocking what was wrong and what was right. I realized I would have lost my daughter if the police had found drugs in my house, something I'd never taken into account due to my ignorance. They easily could have made an example of me, as they did to so many other women trapped within the judicial system—I would have been guilty by association.

Although I was traumatized by the experience, I learned from it. It was time for me to come to terms with new concepts that were rolling through my brain: *Mont'ique, you're a mother before you're a girlfriend. You're a mother before shopping sprees and nice cars. The only loyalty you should be conveying is to that little girl who calls you Mom.* It didn't matter what I had to lose or give up as long as I had my baby girl and she was safe and happy. I focused on being a better mother, and I used my natural hustle and loyalty to establish a solid career that would make my daughter proud.

First, I figured out how to use what confined me to empower me. Providing the opportunity for my daughter to grow taught me more about myself. I discovered I loved to share and serve, and that began to point me toward my purpose-path. Then my godfather, a fire captain at our local fire department, called and told me the department was looking for more women to apply.

At first I thought, *"He's crazy! I'm not going into anyone's burning building,"* but my godfather was very persistent. I didn't know a thing about firefighting, but I began to research the position. The more I learned, the more I desired it. It was a *career*, not just a job, and it would give me structure, hold me accountable, provide benefits for my daughter and me, and give me security for retirement. I applied, and as I trained for the entrance exam, I began to learn my strengths and weaknesses, mentally and physically. This journey was taking me into the deeper depths of who I was on the inside.

For so long, I had allowed men to define me and manipulate me. I needed this opportunity to prove to myself and show my daughter I am strong, capable, and independent. Little did I know, I was on my way from being controlled by men to having men under my command. The thing I had been allowing to control me was actually suppressing my superpower. *I am a leader!* I learned I am creative, bold, confident, and a critical thinker; I can act and plan under pressure.

Growing from a place of rebellion and disregard of authority to newfound respect and honor for leadership is what keeps me in a place of humility and gives me compassion and empathy for those I lead. There is not one piece of my life— good, bad, or indifferent—that isn't a contributing factor to my success.

I love people and enjoy serving and helping others. If you are wondering what does this have to do with mental wealth, I can tell you: It's everything for me. There is no doubt that the cliché When we know better, we do better is true. Once I got my mind right and my focus in proper alignment, I made better decisions when it came to a healthy diversity of relationships, commitments, and desires. I learned to be more deliberate and calculated in my thought process, which lead me onto a path of success.

Many of us can manifest our success by using what we learned from our own life experiences. It's up to us to use those experiences to remind us of what to do or not to do, or as a tool to keep us going no matter how tired we become or how far off our goal seems to be.

We don't need to be struck by lightning or be bitten by a rare spider to develop our superpowers and succeed. We were created for a purpose and there is a God-ordained plan for our destiny. Our strengths and our blueprints for our success are already inside us, but too many of us *never look inside and realize our potential.*

Though as people we're similar, we each have our own priceless superpower, our own version of mental wealth. Our specific superpower is just as different and understandable as having our own fingerprint; there's not another in the entire world like it. That's what makes it our lethal weapon.

*Accept this*: Nobody but you has your power; you are the *only* one who can do it the way you do it. Stay original. Find your passion and go for it! Encourage yourself to never quit. There is a priceless thing inside our treasure box screaming wealth, but we take it for granted most of the time. I quickly learned my passion is teaching others to overcome their fears and manifest the purpose they have within.

I encourage you to see your life and all you were exposed to, all that is around you, and all that is connected to you. Write these things down and trace the true value in each one. Take another look at each person you consider your friend, each person who is close to you. Is the relationship edifying and helpful to your purpose?

Then look at yourself. What are your skills and areas of knowledge? What do you know about yourself? How can these attributes help you succeed?

If you want to identify your mental wealth, then you must begin with identifying what is suppressing your superpower. Develop a strategy to use what was holding you back to now motivate you and catapult you into your destiny.

Before we can go out and gain financial wealth, or even change the world, first we must learn who we are and why we are, revealing our true self to ourselves. It's not what we think that makes us prosperous, it's the undeniable truth about what we know.

# Author's Notes

As a 16-year veteran fire lieutenant, I've faced a variety of challenges regarding race, gender equality, and the ability to lead in a male-dominated field. In the face of what should have made me quit and give up, I prevailed and elevated my purpose.

These experiences helped shape me and propel me into my purpose of being a servant leader. I believe you get the best results when you lead people not with fear or judgment, but with love, compassion, and empathy.

As a Professional Certified Leader, I have gone from following the leader to leading the room. I was CEO and visionary of Elite Pole and Fitness LLC, encouraging and challenging women to establish fitness goals and stay committed to them. I served as a dance team coach, where I not only taught dance but mentored youth by teaching life skills and establishing educational goals. For years, I continued this work as a volunteer with Black Girls Run as the Connecticut Ambassador.

I'm an ordained minister, and also the CEO/founder of All Things God Inc., a charitable organization focused on social being and philanthropy. The organization was born as a hub to house a chain of ministries that support, motivate, inspire, lead, and catapult all people into their virtuous postures. Our proven track record can be found in the testimony of people who did not just experience a conference, have a plate of food, or hear an encouraging word from us, but whose ministry, business, ideas, or goals took a leap of faith and prospered from their All Things God experience.

My mission in this ministry is to assist all people to obtain and fulfill all the things God has predestined for their lives, and most importantly, help them thrive.

I've received the 100 Women of Color award along with citations from the State of Connecticut for my community work as well as ministering and leading women worldwide in my workshops, women conferences, live video Bible talks on social media, and my international *All Things God* podcast.

Of my many awards, recognitions, and citations, the one I hold closest to my heart is the City of Bridgeport's Recognition Award for saving the life of a 10-month-old-child.

I live in West Haven, Connecticut, with Anthony, my beloved husband of ten years, and my two God-sent daughters, Tatyana and Skylyn.

## Contact Information:

**Email:** Honeybeefearless@gmail.com
**Website:** www.allthingsgod.org
**Facebook:** honeybeefearless
**Instagram**: @allthingsgodinc
**Podcast:** All Things God

Chapter 5

# Listen With Confidence

## Heather Monahan

I have trained myself to listen. I'm not saying listening is easy or that it comes naturally to me; it definitely does not. I've trained myself to listen because I've learned a powerful fact: When people feel they are really and truly heard, the dopamine in their brain activates and they begin to feel happier. When people feel cheerful, they are more likely to work in harmony to find a solution.

Listening also signals respect, and respect can mean everything to some people.

A couple of years ago, I was called into a meeting at my son's school to address an issue with his behavior. While meetings like these are never fun, they have taught me a tremendous amount about dealing with adversity and growing as a person.

When you walk into a meeting, especially one that might become adversarial, it's easy to let your emotions get the better of you. There is no place for emotion in meetings; the one who shows emotion is the one who loses. I work to calm my breathing and focus on my strategy.

My strategy is to always let the other party "empty their cup" first. Once you do this, you have information to work from, and information empowers you. Heading into a meeting with your guns blazing or your mind filled with assumptions will leave you upset in the end. Very rarely will be you happy with the outcome.

> There is no place for emotion in meetings; the one who shows emotion is the one who loses.

I calmed myself, sat down, and did not speak.

Remaining calm and not speaking is not easy. It takes practice and discipline, but when you have a goal in mind, employing the right strategy is key to yielding the result you want. I let the school officials share their position, give me their opinions, and talk as much as they wanted to. People like to hear themselves talk. That is a fact of life. Let them. Let them feel heard. Gain information and position yourself to be empowered; it works every single time.

I could sense my cheeks getting hot. At this point in my life, very rarely do I allow myself to get emotional, with the sole exception of issues around my son, Dylan.

The people in our lives who mean the most to us always have the power to put us in very emotional states in trying times. I forced myself to remain calm and quiet.

Starting the meeting by absorbing all the information the other party has to share puts you in a position of power. I recommend this approach whenever you are walking into a difficult negotiation or meeting. When you enter a similar meeting where there is a potential challenge or disagreement, set yourself up for success by encouraging them to talk by asking them for their thoughts or opinions. Repeat back some of what they say; it helps to keep communication clear and let them know you have been actively listening. Don't say, "I hear you," though, because it does not mean you're listening. It's just an acknowledgment, and the phrase is trite and over-used.

At my school meeting, I listened with courtesy, with confidence, without defensiveness, and with encouraging questions. When they were finished, I was ready to begin.

My goal for this meeting was to ensure my son would be set up for success after I left the office that day. Now that I had heard their position, I was able to clearly see the path for me to achieve my goal. There are a number of ways to arrive at that outcome. It is up to us to see the dots and connect them in the best way possible. I saw the dots, and as I began speaking and asking follow-up questions, I began connecting them. Prior to walking into that meeting, I didn't know exactly what the solution would be, but I did know we could find one.

I started with the first observation from one of the teachers, that Dylan had responded aggressively to a specific situation while he was in her class. What struck me as odd was the teachers hadn't discussed or even alluded to the original situation that ignited this chain reaction with my son. *I* knew what the situation was because I had talked with my son in preparation for this meeting.

That looked like a good dot to connect, so I said something to the effect of, "When we began this conversation today, you started with an example of my son acting aggressively. Can you tell me, in your opinion, what elicited that reaction?"

I was confident and relaxed, because I already knew the answer, and asking her the question forced her to own the facts. Asking questions is an extremely powerful tactic. Asking questions you already know the answer to is an even more powerful tactic. The teacher explained that another boy had said something very cruel about my son on a public school forum.

Asking follow-up questions is a powerful course of action, so I said calmly, "Can we please pause for a moment, because I want to point out that *I'd* feel very angry if a peer of mine did that. Is that behavior allowed at school?".

Of course, mean-spirited behavior is not allowed at school, and she agreed that it was an issue. Next, I asked, "How do you think Dylan could have handled it better?"

"He should have called a teacher for help," she said.

That was my opening. Using an opportunity to gain knowledge and then finding ways to have the other person share their opinions allows you to connect the dots.

My logical follow-up question was, "How often *do* fifth-grade boys tell the teacher on each other?"

His teacher admitted, "I don't see that happen often, but I really wish that kids would tell me instead of handling it themselves." That gave me the opportunity to share information with her that she didn't know.

I explained, "We've worked with Dylan to learn to stand up for himself so that he's equipped to handle problems when there isn't a teacher or adult around. It's a strategy that we've worked on for a year. We all know that as we grow, our strategies and abilities evolve and develop. In theory, some things may work, but in reality often different and more realistic tactics or strategies are needed."

The teachers knew I had listened to them with respect, and they listened to me in turn. There wasn't a hint of adversarial attitude or negativity, and we all showed some empathy.

The meeting went on for an hour. We went back and forth between hearing how the school wanted things to be vs. putting ourselves in my son's shoes and discussing what is more realistic.

In the end, we all left the meeting feeling as though my son's motives and actions were now fully understood. So much good can come from being listened to and understood!

Listening signals respect, and it changes the atmosphere in the room. Especially if the others are criticizing you, *listen*. Don't be defensive—just listen. When I said my cheeks were getting hot in my school meeting, they were flaming. My son was being criticized—and by extension, that included me. I sat and listened with respectful confidence, not defensiveness. When it was my turn to talk, the first thing out of my mouth was a question, not a defensive statement. I handled the criticism well by not responding to it and diverted the conversation to problem-solving.

How you deal with criticism is very important, and it leads to a long-term benefit: Handling criticism well will boost your confidence in the long run—and *that's* a game-changer. Confidence is the one thing that changes everything in the environment. When you listen with confidence, you can embrace collaboration and contribute your own ideas.

I wrote the best-selling book, *Confidence Creator,* to share what I've learned on the subject. As a young woman in a male-dominated part of the corporate world, I had to develop confidence quickly to survive, much less thrive.

A good part of my life is now spent helping other people learn confidence. Yes, it can be learned. Building confidence is exactly like training a muscle that can be built up or depleted; it just depends on the actions you take. You always either build your confidence or chip away at it with every action you take. Once you realize that building confidence in yourself is not only attainable but entirely up to you, you're empowered.

*You have this.*

So, let's take a more confident look at a situation you're dealing with right now, something that isn't going the way you want.

Is it on the wrong track because everyone involved doesn't fully understand the situation?

Is it because *you* don't have enough information?

Listen with confidence. Don't be defensive. Gain the knowledge and insight you need.

Only then, *after* you've listened and asked questions, confidently share your perspective and opinion.

You will find a way to agree on a solution.

There is *always* a solution. It's just up to us to find it.

# Author's Notes

As the founder and CEO of Boss in Heels, I am an entrepreneur. I'm also well-known as a confidence expert, keynote and TEDx speaker, and a best-selling author. My recent book, Confidence Creator, shot to number one on Amazon's Business Biography and Business Motivation best-seller lists the first week it was published.

I earned a B.A. in Psychology at Clark University in Worcester, Massachusetts, and began my career as a brand manager at Gallo Wine before I transitioned into broadcasting. After successfully climbing the corporate ladder for nearly 20 years, I was appointed Chief Revenue Officer for Beasley Media Group and was named one of the Most Influential Women in Radio in 2017.

After 14 years of success and continuous advancement, I was unexpectedly fired by another woman. That was one of my lowest moments and forced me to re-evaluate where I was gaining my confidence from. As I began to reflect, I realized that if I was going to start over as a rookie somewhere, I was going to double down on myself. That is when I made the decision to write and self-publish my first book, *Confidence Creator*, and go to work for myself. In 2018, I was named a Limit Breaking Female Founder by Thrive Global. Next, I launched my podcast *Creating Confidence* and landed on the Apple Podcast top 200 list. Then I was named a Top 40 Female Speaker in 2020 by Real Leaders. Today, my clients include Fortune 500 Companies and professional sports franchises, and I help their employees and clients develop confidence in the workplace and on the court.

I'm also very active in my southern Florida community. I was given the honor of receiving the 2015 Glass Ceiling Award from the Florida Women's Conference, recognizing my leadership excellence in the workplace. I'm also a member of Florida International University's Advisory Council, serving as a mentor and leader in the South Florida Community.

My son, Dylan, and I live in Miami.

## Contact Information

**Website:** heathermonahan.com
**Facebook:** Heather Monahan Official
**Instagram:** @Heather Monahan
**Twitter:** @_heathermonahan

# Chapter 6

# Your Outlook Determines Your Outcome

### Bjorn "Beez" Hendricks

*Fear is not real. The only place that fear can exist is in our thoughts of the future. It is the product of our imagination, causing us to fear things that do not at present and may not ever exist. That is near insanity.*

*Now do not misunderstand me, danger is very real, but fear is a choice.*

—**Will Smith, as Cypher Raige** in *After Earth*

Have you ever dreamed of something you could not attain, no matter how much you wanted it? Maybe you even started working toward your dream, but at some point life interrupted you, and you missed one day, then another, then a week—maybe even two weeks. I am here to tell you that you are *not* alone. *Habit* and *fear* are just two of the many concepts that keep us from achieving our goals. But they all fall into one primary category—mindset.

## Mindset

Your outlook determines your outcome. Fear is a mental construct that holds us back from achieving so much. We often say negative things to frighten ourselves:

*What if it doesn't work out?*
*It's too difficult for me!*
*If I don't try, I won't fail.*

It particularly hurts me when I hear people say that last sentence. They're forgetting that if they don't try, they will *never* succeed.

> *The epitome of mental wealth is always learning and trying to improve.*

Every one of these statements is a figment of our imagination, our own creation. *We* put those ideas into our own heads. *We* let those ideas fester and grow. Most of us eventually let our fear prevent us from taking the first (or next) step on our path of greatness. We are allowing an imaginary construct to define our journey and our destiny.

A concept I regularly promote to my students is the ability to *unlearn* and then *relearn*, which can be a daunting task, but is vital to our growth. While we are the sum of our experiences at this moment, it doesn't mean our past must define our future. If we open our minds to thinking from a different perspective, we open ourselves to limitless possibilities.

### Our mindset matters

You may have heard the rumor that Charles Holland Duell, the former Commissioner of the U.S. Patent Office, said more than 100 years ago, *Everything that can be invented has already been invented.*

The rumor has been debunked and attributed to an 1899 edition of *Punch Magazine* where someone else was quoted. However, let's seriously look at those words. They were said before airplanes were invented—or the television! Definitely before computers. Primitive cars were just being produced. That is a small example of the power of mindset and how perception can change the world.

Imagine if such a narrow-minded belief had been commonplace at the time. The wonders of the 20th century that paved the way for how we live our lives may have never come to fruition. We should always tell ourselves *anything* is possible! We have so much we can achieve in our short existence, and it *all* starts with having the correct mindset to believe we *can* do it.

### Why?

When I was presented with the opportunity to contribute to this book, I was equally elated and empowered. The project forced me to sit down and have an internal conversation with my authentic self. I asked myself, *What does mental wealth really mean to me?*

You may have heard the saying: *Success is when opportunity meets preparation.* To me, it's a little more complex: *Success is when opportunity meets preparation and speed!* What do I mean by that? Well, procrastination is another consequence of our mindset, a result of letting fear control our actions, tell us what we can't do, and literally hold us back.

Let me give you an example of an opportunity presented to me just a few days ago. Les Brown and Johnny Wimbrey spoke at a conference and mentioned an opportunity for the right person to co-author a book on a future project. Before I left the conference, I contacted Johnny's team and submitted my application. After they met with me and heard my background, I was invited to work with them on a book that would be released in 2022. They said it was a shame the deadline had just passed on *The Power of Mental Wealth*, because my expertise would have been a perfect fit.

You could have heard the wheels turning in my head.

Many have assumed I was born with the ability to identify turning points in my life—forks in the road—but it's something I've developed with much care over the years. This was definitely one of those forks! I asked, "What would it take to get into *The Power of Mental Wealth?*"

When I was told it would take a miracle, I didn't hesitate to ask for details of the miracle and any problems that might be in my way.

**Opportunity**: The chance to co-author a book with Les Brown, Johnny Wimbrey, and Heather Monahan. I could *not* pass that up!

**Preparation**: I'm always seeking and learning information, and it gives me the experience, ability, and confidence to write about my topic at length.

**Speed**: I was told that the project was wrapping up to go to press, and I'd have no more than three to four days to write my chapter and get it to the editors so they could meet the book launch deadline.

Now ask yourself, what would *you* say if you were told you had three days to write a chapter of an important book? Would you say, "That's not enough time!" Or perhaps say, "I already have other plans I can't change." Or would you just wait until next year?

Since tomorrow is never promised, we must always keep in our mindset that *we can accomplish anything today* rather than waiting for another day. If we don't even try, we definitely will never achieve our goals.

Mindset! This is the start of our accumulation of mental wealth and the power it provides us.

*So many people spend their health gaining wealth, and then have to spend their wealth to regain their health.*
**—A.J. Reb Materi, Canadian Catholic clergyman**

### Defining wealth

If you search online for the meaning of *wealth*, a good definition is from Investopedia: *Wealth measures the value of all the assets of worth owned by a person, community, company, or country.*

Now take a moment and think back carefully. When a discussion has come up about wealth in your past, in what direction does the conversation always seem to veer? I am willing to bet that you said *financial wealth* to yourself just now. Actually, there are five:

**Financial wealth**: *Money*. Money is, of course, the most common form of wealth people discuss, but many would argue it is one of the least important.

**Physical wealth**: *Health*. The state of your physical health is probably the second most common version, yet it's too often overlooked. Many entrepreneurs sacrifice their health only to see its value once they obtain financial wealth. Without health, we can't endure the stress and trials we suffer through as we continue to build our financial wealth.

**Time wealth**: *Freedom*. My personal favorite. Time wealth is what caused me to leave my six-figure corporate career at Microsoft. Though I was already well on my way in my financial wealth journey, I did not own my time. If my son had a basketball game, or my daughter had a dance recital, I had to beg for my own time back so that I could attend—and it was not always granted.

This even occurs in the world of entrepreneurs who think they have finally reclaimed their time since they "work for themselves." Robert Kyosaki introduces the cash-flow quadrant concept in his book *Rich Dad, Poor Dad*. He explains that we need to stop trading our *time for money*; instead, we should trade *results for money*.

When you're an employee or self-employed, you are typically trading your time for money, but when you move to the business owner or investor quadrants, your results generate the money.

**Social Wealth**: *Status*. At first glance, you may think status holds the least value, but I challenge you to think again.

In 2020, real estate mogul Grant Cardone participated in *Undercover Billionaire*, a Discovery channel show. He was dropped in a remote town without his fortune, name, or any resources beyond a beat-up old car and $100, with the challenge of creating a million-dollar business in just 90 days. What do you think was the first thing Grant did as the challenge began? He decided he needed to know who the movers and shakers in the town were because the power of networking is *priceless*. If you are around the right people, the opportunities will flow toward you. Social wealth feeds into every other form of wealth.

Remember this as you read the chapter: *Wealth can be contrasted to income, in that wealth is a stock and income is a flow.* The statement can be seen in either absolute or relative terms. So what term would I use to define mental wealth?

**Mental Wealth: *Wisdom*.** During my corporate career, when I was trying to improve operations at large firms, I often looked at different types of process management methodologies, and found knowledge management was key. Within that field, there is the **DIKW** model/pyramid, which demonstrates how we improve our level of understanding as we add context to data:

**Data**. A collection of facts in a raw and unorganized form.

**Information**. Adding the context of *what* (or *who, when, where*) to the data brings us to a higher level of understanding.

**Knowledge**. As we continue to add context, we now look at the *how*. How is the data relevant to our goals? How can we apply the information to achieve our goals? How does this connect to other information so we can add more value and meaning?

**Wisdom**. Now we get to the *why,* which is at the top of the DIKW pyramid. First, we answer questions, such as "why do something," and "which course of action is best." At this level, you're moving your knowledge from the previous level into action!

So, if wealth is *stock*, or accumulation of something, and mental wealth equates to *wisdom*, then you can deduce that mental wealth has a lot to do with the accumulation of wisdom. The epitome of mental wealth is always learning and trying to improve.

*Wisdom* doesn't mean just intelligence or book learning. Wisdom can be as simple as coming to the realization that *fear is not real and only exists in our thoughts of the future.*

Now, do you see where I'm going with this?

**Growth**

When it comes to creating financial wealth in this world, there are only three major financial vehicles you can use:

**Real estate**. A tried-and-true method that stands the test of time. Some of the richest people in history amassed their wealth by accumulating property.

**The financial markets**. Includes stocks and the like, and is another great way to diversify your portfolio.

**Building a business.** Where I spend most of my efforts. You can create far more wealth for yourself when *you're* the one who started the business—much more so than investing in someone else's business.

We can see now that amassing wealth in finance is similar to amassing mental wealth. Look at real estate for an analogy: While fix-and-flips are great for short-term profit, it's the buy-and-hold strategy that creates generational wealth.

We need to use the buy-and-hold strategy when acquiring wisdom. We should keep investing in our minds by attaining more knowledge, eventually transition this knowledge into wisdom, and aim to diversify the knowledge we acquire. We will always grow our mental wealth faster when we shift our thinking and understand we are *investing in ourselves!*

As any good financial planner will tell us, it's important to periodically evaluate our portfolio to see what can be strengthened. The same goes for our minds.

**Credit**

Because we are comparing mental and financial wealth, let's pivot slightly to discuss credit.

The power and use of credit are fundamental to the Business Builders methodology I developed, which allows you to identify, start, and scale multiple autonomous businesses, where you steer the process instead of operating within it. Credit is vital to this methodology, as it can be used to start and grow any business.

I also preach about the importance of business credit over personal credit. While that concept is worth a separate chapter, you should also understand your personal credit is still necessary as a personal guarantee (PG) when you apply for business credit, so don't neglect your personal credit profile.

*Credit utilization* is just the measure of how much of your available credit you currently use across all your accounts. It makes up 30% of your credit score, second only to your payment history, which is 35% of your score.

It's often said that you should keep your utilization below 30%. That's not a bad percentage, but it doesn't help your credit score. Let's look at this in more detail.

Let's say you have five credit cards with different credit limits. Let's also say that one of those cards has a $2,000 credit limit and the total sum of your credit card limits is $10,000. If you charged $2,000 on that first card, you have utilized 100% of the credit limit on that card. That scenario affects your relationship with that specific credit card issuer, and *may* even lead to the company decreasing your credit limit or canceling your card.

If all your other cards have zero balances, you are still using 20% of your *total* credit limit. It's not bad, but it doesn't increase your score. To have a *positive* effect on your credit score, you need to keep your credit utilization score below 10%; 2%-6% is the optimum goal.

So, what does any of this have to do with the power of mental wealth?

As I have matured over the years, I have realized it's not enough for me to be passive with my mind or body. When I was in my 20s, if I had stopped lifting weights for a month, my body probably wouldn't have changed much. At my current age, if I stop working out for a week, I feel as though I've aged five years and my flab comes back exponentially.

When it comes to your mind, it's the same scenario. As time goes on, it becomes even more urgent for you to nurture your mental wealth. It's not enough to try to just avoid stress or even to simply remove toxicity from your life. The *real* secret is to actively take steps to improve your mind and change your life for the better.

## Unlearn and relearn

If you ever wanted to become an entrepreneur and gain the time freedom I value, one of the best ways to unlearn and relearn is to relate your entrepreneurial journey to your college experience. Ask yourself:

*Why are so many of us willing to live as starving college students for four or more years on the hope of eventually making a middle-class salary? But why, after starting a business with substantially more potential income, are we ready to quit in a few months because we aren't rich yet?*

This question opens our minds to a different perspective. Our lives are not a reflection of the events that happen to us, but a reflection of how we *react* to those events!

*We control our destiny!* We hold the power to live the life we want, but we must be willing to make certain changes. And it all starts with the mental wealth we accumulate.

# Author's Notes

My corporate career focused on information technology management and strategic consultancies, working with Fortune 500 companies, including Accenture and Microsoft, plus several major government agencies. Over the last several years, I made the shift to developing and launching my own multi-million-dollar companies.

Now I'm a successful entrepreneur, known widely for having coined the more powerful and strategic term *Business Builder* to replace *serial entrepreneur*. I'm also known for teaching the Business-Builder methodology to hundreds of students through my Business Builders Institute (BBI) where we focus on financial literacy and ways to improve access to capital. My students have launched many successful, high-earning businesses.

Because my businesses have expanded into multiple service-based niches, I've earned the title of Business Builder Beez. My companies include Capital Beez (financial literacy and business funding); SellerKai (e-commerce supply chain management); Domani Digital (digital marketing); Dominicus Motors (luxury and exotic vehicle rentals and sales); Aytak Solutions (global recruitment and talent acquisition); The Business Builders Institute (entrepreneur education and mentorship); and more.

I'm always passionate about giving back to my community through education on financial literacy, with a focus on building generational wealth. This passion has led me to create HIVE, a social coalition of leaders who work together to improve our communities. I've also co-founded The BAG, Inc. *(Building Assets Generationally)*, a nonprofit focused on helping youth in underserved communities nationwide.

I was born in Jamaica into humble circumstances and grew up in New York. I attended the University of Central Florida, graduating with a degree in Management Information Systems and Computer Science. I hold multiple certifications including Lean IT Expert, CISSP, ITIL Expert, PRINCE 2, and Lean Six Sigma. I'm fluent in Spanish and Mandarin, and enjoy traveling the globe.

I live in Fort Lauderdale, Florida with my amazing four children, Damani, 17, Dominic, 14, and twins Kai and Katya, 7. They are truly the *why* behind all that I do.

# Contact Information

**Email:** Info@thebusinessbuilders.training
**Facebook:** BusinessBuilderBeez
**Instagram:** @BusinessBuilderBeez
**Twitter:** @12figurebeez
**Websites:** sellerkai.com
aytaksolutions.com
getdomani.digital
thebusinessbuilders.training
capitalbeez.com
dominicusmotors.com

Chapter 7

# Success Begins From Within

## Christopher King-Hall

We all have the power to be greater than we ever imagined possible, and it all starts within. Living life as the best version of yourself starts with the belief you can accomplish anything upon which you set your mind and focus. Your mindset becomes the focus, and focus becomes energy. Remember, what you focus on and put energy into, good or bad, will manifest in your life.

My goal is to inspire others to be all they can be and to make the world a better place by generating positivity in people's lives with self-courage and self-love. Our energy is a direct outcome of what we share with other people.

*The power of mental wealth is within you*—it is the power to move our life in any direction. We can choose to be either powerless or the most powerful energy source in our own lives and it all starts with our thought processes.

In this chapter, I share what I believed to be the most powerless time in my life became the most significant and empowering time of my life—a period that would change the trajectory of the rest of my life's journey. My story will give you a glimpse of how I learned, changed, and took control of my health, mindset, belief systems, self-confidence, love, and overall perspective on life. I realized we all can take control of our destiny and shape the life we want to live.

> You are extraordinary, and it all starts from within.

I'm reinventing myself by creating the life I want to live through an active lifestyle and my creative passion to inspire people to want to change the world together. There is a humanitarian paradigm shift happening in front of our eyes and we need to take action to shape a better world for our children and those affected by an impoverished, unjust, and unequal racially charged society. There is a burning desire inside of me to help the people I care about and all people who are struggling to live a better life. We are all brilliant-minded people. There is nothing we can't accomplish when we work together to make the world a better place.

## A Brief History

It's important for you to know my journey so you can understand my perspectives at a personal level. I've always been a fighter. I don't like to give up. Maybe that was instilled in me when my mother's water broke just

26 weeks into her pregnancy. The doctors warned my parents that my chances of living were slim. Two weeks later, I was born, weighing just two pounds, four ounces. I wanted a shot at life, and I'm still here today because something inside me does not give up, no matter what.

I enjoy life's struggles, and I still look for ways to challenge myself because I know I will grow from each experience. When we have goals and bring purpose and passion into our lives, the inner motivation to defy all odds can make us or break us.

My parents divorced when I was three years old, and their separation launched a childhood filled with changes. As a youth, I often believed my upbringing to be unnecessarily challenging and often wondered how my life would have been different if I had been raised like a "normal person." I laugh at that perspective now, because I've learned to look back on my younger years with a great sense of love and appreciation. The changes I faced gave me an understanding of life that is much richer than if I had lived in the small town of St. Albans, Vermont, for my entire life.

During the next 23 years, I lived in 15 different homes in four states. When I was 27, a good buddy and I drove to the west coast from Vermont, hauling our worldly belongings behind us. Both of us wanted to change our lives drastically, and our heads were filled with "California Dreaming." That's exactly what I got.

One year later, I was living in San Francisco in a five-bedroom house with a dozen Vermont friends, and we all had the desire to create art, music, videos, and chase our dreams.

That was before YouTube, by the way.

***Let's backtrack a bit***. My burning desire to create and tell stories through visual experiences sprouted while I studied media productions and photography in high school. In college, I studied film production, and after graduation, I went to work at an ABC News affiliate station as an editor and lighting/production grip for the evening news. It was fun, although I soon realized I could make more money doing non-media jobs.

I left ABC and for five years worked at a hospital as a surgical instrument cleaning technician. This work paid well, but it wasn't my true path, didn't feed my purpose, and did not bring me joy. I took a break for a three-month road trip. When I returned, I knew I had to move to California and chase my creative desires there. To prepare and save up for the move, I worked five simultaneous jobs while completing my film certificate program.

Once I moved to the west coast, I quickly settled into California life and eventually became happily married.

I worked in top hotels as their audiovisual (AV) expert, which led me into the live-event AV world. Eventually, I became Director of Event Technologies at a top-tier hotel in the financial district of San Francisco. It was a job I could have had for life and it would have given me a good retirement. However, I didn't feel as though I had purpose. I liked my work yet I knew I still wasn't on my true life path.

The presenters in the events I managed inspired me when they talked about their visions and world views. There was more to life, and I knew I wanted more. I had always believed I had been born for something greater—something with deeper meaning and purpose.

## Changing priorities and passions

Everyone at the hotel appreciated my work ethic; I worked long hours and was committed to always doing an excellent job. But when my first son was born toward the end of 2014, I soon realized I couldn't maintain that work schedule and be the supportive and nurturing father and husband I wanted to be. In February 2015, after five years as director, I gave my notice. It was a difficult decision and I was nervous. I wanted to provide for my family, yet I was determined to make a change. I needed to be home more, and I wanted a freelance lifestyle so I could choose when I wanted to work.

From the beginning of my freelance career, I worked with fifteen clients on a pretty consistent basis, doing live-event AV work, in full control of my schedule. In 2016, almost exactly one year into my new life and just 14 months after our first child was born, we welcomed a second son into the world. It became even more important to give time and support to my family.

After just two years as a freelancer, I was making as much as I had as a director and I was working only two-thirds as many hours. After five years, I was making almost double what I had made as a director, and I became more selective. I chose to work with a handful of companies and had the flexibility to decide what events I wanted to work.

Life was busy—I felt in control, yet something was still missing. I was still lacking the purpose I craved. I've always dreamed about being able to change the world some way, somehow—but my actions *weren't* creating or impacting people's lives in a positive way. I *wasn't* changing the world. I still needed to pay the bills, and I needed to be responsible to my family. Could I just walk away from my work and just take time to ponder and create? I didn't think so.

At the beginning of 2020, I was fired up and expecting a record-breaking flurry of events and clients for the year. On the first day of January, I had launched my own media company, Rain Sky Media LLC. I'd named the company after my sons not only to honor them and their importance in my life, but also to serve as a daily reminder of why I need to remain motivated. Using just their middle names gave the three of us a shared secret and a constant source of private happiness. I was working with a brilliant new event space in downtown San Francisco, and its team and I had invested years into creating one of the premier venues in the city.

The year started strong—and came to a halt when the COVID-19 virus hit. Within 72 hours, the majority of the events for the entire year had either been canceled or rescheduled. The lives of everyone around the world changed drastically. Within months, all business was gone, California was in lockdown, and I was home with my family, sheltered in place, focusing on our health as the top priority.

It was a difficult time. I took a deep look inside and asked myself, *How can I use this time to my advantage? Where am I in my life and where do I want to go? How can I make this work?* I've always looked at adversity as a time to grow and prosper. Now I was about to embark on a new stage in my life, opening up a new state of mind, putting me on the path to change my life forever.

Being a father in my forties made me aware I needed to take care of my health. With thousands of people dying every day, the pandemic raised my awareness to an entirely new level. During the summer of 2020, I began choosing healthier foods, and committed to exercising every day and getting enough sleep. To keep myself paced for success, I set a goal of running a trail marathon and set aside time to run as much as I could. I completed the marathon on my 43rd birthday in the midst of a 100-day stretch of running every day.

After multiple knee surgeries and a rebuilt ACL, I thought my days as a runner were over. Proper nutrition, patience, and persistence changed all that. By the year's end, I'd run 1,241 miles over 263 days. I can't emphasize enough how important healthy choices are for a longer, more prosperous life. Mental wealth comes literally from within, and it starts with what you put into your body.

Don't place limits on what you think you can accomplish. Set your ambitions higher than you think you can achieve. Make sure your goal-setting aligns with your true passions in life. Make sure you have mentors who inspire you and have accountability partners to keep you on track.

With no work in the middle of the pandemic, it would have been easy for me to focus on the bad and complain all of it was unfair—my finances were hurting and my savings were being drained to pay the bills. But it didn't take me long to realize the most important thing to do was to give thanks and be grateful for little things. Perhaps all of the transitions I made in my young life helped me cope better in times of adversity.

Because of the pandemic, I've learned to be more grateful for everything in life. It's true what the leaders and mentors of the world say: *The more you are grateful in life, the more fulfilling a life you will live, the more the universe will give to you, and the more you can prosper and give back to others.*

Okay, we all have bad days! Some are worse than others, that's for sure. There will be days we wish never happened. Just accept the truth: When bad happens, it could always be worse. Also, accept that life puts us through difficult circumstances—not to punish us or to force pain on us—but because the universe needs us to grow and become stronger so we can endure our *true* life purpose.

Gaining mental control of our thoughts is the key to either truly becoming limitless or doing nothing at all. We set our *own* limits by deciding what we can accomplish. You fail the moment you lose faith in yourself or the instant you tell yourself *I can't do this.*

I'm here to tell you this: *Every time you hear doubt in your head, reverse the thought process.* Don't allow yourself to fail because you believe you can't do something. The power is in *you!* Remember that every challenge or failed attempt is just an opportunity to learn and grow. Thomas Edison attempted to perfect the light bulb ten thousand times before he was successful.

You too are a creator without limits, and it all starts from within.

Our mental focus and daily routines can shape our lives to be more fulfilling and prosperous than we ever imagined, while our belief systems can either empower us or hold us back. How many times have you said to yourself *I can't do this!* because you let a bad memory limit you? Don't let the past control your future.

### A new perspective

The latest transitional period in my life has opened a gateway for me. In summer 2020, my perspective completely changed when I participated in *Unleash The Power Within,* a virtual Tony Robbins event. Tony introduced me to Master Stephen Co, who introduced me to the art of meditation and the appreciation that we are all beings of divine light and energy. I feel self-reflection and meditation are truly empowering arts, and they help anyone have a great sense of purpose and self-appreciation. I encourage everyone to take time out whenever they can to explore the possibilities in meditation and enrich their life journey.

Every one of us has a purpose in life, a destiny. Now I also see *we have to believe in ourselves*. We have the power to mold our lives to become what we want them to be. Ask yourself what is more painful for you—leaving this life knowing you could have given it more or challenging yourself to give it all you have to give? Start today, take charge, and make a decision that will springboard you in a new direction of your dreams.

I am grateful for every experience in my life, and I truly believe each challenge was a chance to grow. There are no decisions I regret or experiences I didn't deserve. All of my experiences, good and bad, created who I am today. All of the choices we make have consequences, and we must experience them before we're able to fulfill our life's destiny.

Life is a continuous journey and we shouldn't treat it like a destination. Staying hungry and striving for the next goal in life will create a belief system and appreciation for life that can be limitless and continually gratifying.

No matter the odds, *don't give up*. Simply taking responsibility for your expectations and your reactions can absolutely give you power beyond your wildest dreams. Remember, you are extraordinary and it all starts from within. No matter what your talents, you can contribute to the world.

The only difference between being ordinary and extraordinary is your mindset and belief in yourself. Don't ever lose confidence in yourself. Don't let the beliefs of others bring you down or convince you that you are not capable of something great—*especially* if that is something that you're passionate about.

Are you ordinary? No, you are extraordinary!

You are a creator.

# Author's Notes

My background is in video production, customer service, and live event audio-visual services; I call myself a visual storyteller.

Born and reared in Vermont, I live in Northern California. I'm a proud husband to Yi, and the father of two young boys, now five and six years old. Being a father and having a loving and supportive wife has created an immense feeling of love and appreciation in my life. I could not have survived this journey and especially these difficult times without the unwavering love and support of my wife.

Although I've lived a full life, my true journey and purpose in life are just beginning. My chapter is a glimpse into my life story and how the last 12 months have put me on a journey of purpose with a limitless mindset. My goal is to inspire you, so when you believe in yourself and you take action to create your dreams, anything is possible.

Be well, stay amazing, and remember you have the power within! Let's change the world together.

# Contact Information

**Email:** rainskymediallc@gmail.com
**Website:** http://rainskymedia.com/
**Instagram:** christopherkinghall

# Chapter 8

# It's Okay to Ask For Help

### Jayln Nicola

I was so sure 2020 would be *my* year. The year before, I'd dedicated my life to the Lord, whom I call Papa, and I knew He would help me with the difficult transition I'd started.

I would never have predicted what happened next—one of the toughest times in history, with a pandemic paralyzing the entire world. For the first couple of months, I was able to stay home with Raquel, my wife, ensuring she was well protected because of her underlying health conditions. All too soon, I received a call from the National Guard that would change my life as I knew it. I was to join the fight against COVID-19 in New York City.

Though I had been deployed around the world during my 20 years in the 101$^{st}$ Airborne and the New York National Guard, my new deployment was definitely more dangerous. I had never been in a situation where the enemy was invisible to the naked eye. I arrived in Manhattan, where I would be working for more than a year, and the first thing I did was go to my office and thank Papa for all He had done for me up until that moment. Then I asked Him to help me through my suffering.

What do I mean by that?

I am a transgender man, and I had decided to live the life I was meant to live. I began my transition in late 2018 with hormones. On the day I received my first testosterone injection, Jennifer Nicola died and Jayln Nicola was born. Not everyone in my immediate circle of friends and family understood, but most were supportive. I had my first surgery scheduled, but unfortunately it had to be postponed because of my COVID-19-related deployments.

> One of the more subtle additions to my life is learning to forgive myself.

I battled gender dysphoria for many years. I knew there was something different about me from a very young age. When I was in sixth grade, I was timid and isolated from everyone, and always felt uncomfortable. I didn't want to be just one of the girls. I wanted to be one of the *guys*.

Because I felt I could relate better with the guys, I started hanging with them. Not much later, I started dating girls, and it felt so natural. I met my wife when I was 19, and we have been together ever since. We have four beautiful children and three godchildren.

I had wanted to be in the military since I was a small child; it is all I wanted to be. I enlisted in the Army when I was just eighteen, purely coincidentally on September 11, 2001. Despite the *Don't Ask, Don't Tell* policy in effect for my first ten years, I'd always thrived in the service. While I didn't "tell," I also didn't hide my sexual orientation. As a lesbian, I'd worked my way up to E7, or Master Sergeant, in the New York National Guard. My responsibilities include overseeing our dining halls and inspecting facilities at other bases.

When I deployed to Manhattan to manage food services for COVID-19 patients, no one in my unit knew I had begun my transition to being male. The hormones were seriously affecting me in every way, emotionally as well as physically. Side effects include severe anxiety, weight gain, depression, and hypertension. I felt freaking miserable, ungainly, cranky, and unhappy. My body was changing, but so was my mind.

At the same time, I was working 20 hours a day, trying to do the impossible, responsible for feeding hundreds of infected people, as my transitioning body was fighting me in all sorts of new ways. I never knew how it was going to react. Everything was exacerbated by the fact I was alone, away from my wife and family, my entire support system. When I learned my surgeries had to be postponed because of my deployment, I was devastated—and angry.

My deployments to Iraq and Afghanistan had been stressful, but nothing like this. Of course, the fact that I was quietly transitioning without any of my troops or superiors knowing and having just three to four hours of sleep per day were the rogue cards in the deck.

There were days I'd say to myself *I can't let my soldiers see me this way* and I'd race to my office so nobody would catch a glimpse of me in crisis. I never asked for help. It's not that I didn't believe in people asking for help; I was always willing and able to help and counsel my troops. I'd mentored and counseled at least 1,000 soldiers since I'd had a suicidal stretch of my own years before, but I would not, *could not,* accept help from anyone else. Whenever I needed someone, I talked myself out of it by convincing myself no one was available.

I'd suck it up and suffer anxiety attacks alone, away from my family, living in a hotel, working unbearable hours a day—right until the day my body and my mind couldn't take it anymore. I almost passed out. My blood pressure was through the roof. I knew I was dying. Finally, I called for one of my soldiers and she came to my aid.

At that point, I was scared, certain I was about to die, but I knew I didn't want to die alone. That's the only thing that made it through my mind at that moment. With my soldier's help, I made it to the hospital, absolutely convinced I was about to make the really big transition.

When I learned my anxiety had triggered a severe panic attack, I realized I'd heard about this from my niece, Ladyann, who'd suffered from debilitating anxiety and depression. She had told me, "Tio, you have no idea what this feels like! It's the worst feeling in the world." Several times she actually said, "I'm going to die from this."

Unfortunately, she was right.

But I didn't know it then. Instead, I'd minimize her pain and say, "Ladyann, stop talking like that!" In my head, I would ask myself *how bad could this really be?* Well, let me tell you, I found out very quickly how bad it was. I regret Ladyann died before I could tell her I finally understood what she was going through.

Once that first COVID-19 deployment was complete, I went home for a month of rest. But all too soon, I received another phone call from the National Guard, and I was placed on orders again. In my second Manhattan COVID-19 deployment, my workload and responsibility grew from responsibility for feeding hundreds of people a day to feeding a few thousand a day. My job was to ensure everyone had four meals to eat. As the numbers grew, so did my anxiety.

Once I realized work-related stress and hormone-triggered anxiety was. my new normal and it wasn't going away, I started researching how I could handle it better. *Finally*, my mind was open to receiving help. I decided to handle it by investing in myself. I really like the way Johnny Wimbrey describes this process in his new book, *Building A Millionaire Mindset*: **"I participated in my own rescue."**

Once I decided to rescue myself, I was determined to work with the very best at what they do. I made my first promise to myself when I committed to making a very substantial investment, and it's changed my life. I was finally willing to ask myself what I really needed and wanted.

That's why I was receptive when I started to work with Les Brown, one of the best motivational speakers in the world. He gave me the confidence to follow my dreams, helped me recognize some of the obstacles holding me back, and he taught me how to organize my thoughts better. He also started me in a new habit of listening to a variety of other motivational speakers.

One morning I was listening to *The Best Motivational Speeches of 2019* as I exercised, and I'm sure fate intervened to make sure I extended my workout just so I could hear Lisa Nichols' story.

Lisa told listeners that she'd been in an abusive relationship, one so bad that she had lost herself. She finally went to a therapist, who told Lisa she was clinically depressed and should be on medication. Lisa asked the therapist, "May I try something on my own for the next 30 days? I promised if it doesn't work, I'll take the medications you want to give me."

The therapist agreed, and Lisa went home and started taping affirmations all over the walls of her house. She would read each of them every day. At the end of the month, the therapist was amazed at Lisa's results and her improved state of mind. She said to Lisa, "Whatever you did on your own, it's working. May I borrow your method for my patients?"

As I was listening to Lisa speak, I started getting emotional. She spoke about her dad taking her on her "first date." He bought her dinner, and he opened the car door for her. At the end of the evening, Lisa's dad opened the front door of their home for her, but then stopped her from going in the house and said, "Lisa, tonight I took you on your 'first date' so you get to see how you *should* be treated. Now, sweetheart, how you *choose* to get treated, that's going to be on *you*."

At that moment I decided I really needed to change, just for me.

Then I found Mel Robbins and her course, *Mindset Reset*. When I read what she wrote, it felt as though she'd written it just for me: *You are tired of feeling stressed. Life is overwhelming. Ready for some serious change?*

Mel designed a free 35-day program that starts with some self-evaluation, and then she emailed daily exercises I had to complete. That got me started on a positive track. I also began to meditate morning and evening. Sometimes the emotional stress was so powerful I needed to meditate many times throughout the day.

Soon I added Jon Talarico of The Power Voice, who specializes in building relationships. I learned how to find my opportunities and then use a network of connections to build a better life. His theme is "anything is possible."

Now I'm also working with Bob Proctor of The Proctor Gallagher Institute, who helped me find a new purpose in life and wake up each day excited to learn and grow.

I've been learning about investing in the stock market from Darren Winters, and working with Forbes Riley to hone my "pitch."

These powerful and talented individuals have also taught me how to control my anxiety in ways that give me positive energy. James McNeil has been my mentor for meditation. Meditating twice a day is my goal, and I meet it more and more often. I take care of myself in physical ways, as well. I've been exercising, drinking tons of water, and avoiding alcohol.

One of the more subtle additions to my life is learning to forgive myself. My life has changed for the better. And all because I finally realize that even those of us who help others need to be helped ourselves.

As I reached out, I began realizing what I needed the most and I asked for it: *Papa, please align me with the people who out-think me.*

And sure enough, it's just like Steve Harvey says, "You have not because you ask not." Once I asked, I got.

I asked for mentors and individuals who would hold me accountable for my actions. I was soon aligned with Gary Cowan, a gentleman who would most definitely hold me accountable, no matter how hard I tried to wriggle out of it.

I was also aligned with Kenson Charles, who has become a great friend. Kenson is a straightforward guy who doesn't care if you like him or not. More than once he's told me I need to get my crap together. Kenson is also the guy who pulled me aside and said seriously, "Listen, if you do this, your life will be easier, and it will get better."

I've worked hard to rescue myself, and I've invested a great deal of energy, time, and money. The key takeaway I want to share with you in this chapter is this: *It's okay to ask for help.*

When you suffer in silence, not only is your judgment clouded, but your health is compromised. Even worse—you can actually die from your silence and solitude. Don't allow the gifts you were given to die with you. Have faith that you were meant for more, that you have a purpose you are meant to fulfill. Pull out the champion who is inside of you to push you through the hard times. As Les Brown says, "That's my story and I'm sticking to it."

# Author's Notes

As Jennifer Nicola, I was born in Long Island, New York. Now, as Jayln, I reside in New York City with my wife Raquel Rodriguez when I'm not deployed. We have four wonderful children and a beloved godchild. I studied com-puter engineering and networking at Briarcliff College, and business administration at Colorado Technical University.

The Army and National Guard are a major part of my adult life. I enrolled as a private into the 501$^{st}$ Signal Battalion of the 101$^{st}$ Airborne Brigade, and performed the duties of a Culinary Specialist from 2001 to 2009. After leaving the Army, I continued my military career by enlisting in the New York Army National Guard in 2009, and am still serving to this date as a Food Unit Leader, Sergeant First Class.

My awards and decorations include the Combat Action Badge, Army Commendation Medal with one oak leaf cluster, Iraq Service Ribbon, and Afghanistan Service Ribbon. I'm most proud, though, of having mentored more than 1,000 soldiers.

I plan to continue actively mentoring after I leave military service. Preparing for that time, in every spare moment I'm working on self-improvement and developing the skills I'll need to be a successful entrepreneur.

In addition to the mentors and teachers I mentioned previously, I want to thank my physician, Dr. Dean Miller. He's not only been an amazing doctor, he's also been an amazing friend. When I first told him I planned to transition to male, he said, "I have never had a patient go through this; however, whatever I can do to help you finally become the man you want to become, I will do it." Dr. Miller was the first to support my decision, after my wife and youngest daughter Cierra, and I borrowed and adopted his phrase, "the man you want to become."

I would like to dedicate this chapter to Anibal Ventura, my loving uncle, a man who was like a father to me. He, unfortunately, passed due to COVID-19, but his last words to me were, "I never said this before, but I'm so proud of you. You stuck it out and didn't care what anyone said about you. Don't let anyone hold you back, *ever!*"

# Contact Information

**Email:** Jnicola1976@gmail.com
**Facebook:** Jayln Nicola
**Instagram:** Jayln Nicola

## Chapter 9

# Keep Your Chin Up And Stand Tall!

**Dolores C. Macias**

When I was young, I swallowed a bitter pill that made me believe I was born only to endure barbaric curve balls thrown at me in the game of life. By the time I was 15, I was married, and when I was 19, I'd had my two kids and my tubes were tied. Two years later, my husband abandoned the three of us 1,300 miles from our hometown.

After another year went by, I began living with Benny, a wonderful, loving 18-year-old Mexican guy who spoke no English and who had a fourth-grade education. Two months passed, and I told him, "I'm going home to my mama and papa. Do you want to go with me?"

Benny's family thought he was crazy to move so far away with an older married lady with two little kids. Even worse, his family was very outspoken about my tubes being tied, saying it was a disgrace to the Mexican culture that he couldn't have children of his own if he went with me. But we packed the car, the four of us got in, and we left everything else behind with no regrets.

He worked hard, paid for my divorce, married me, loved me and my two kids, Monica and Rick, and adopted them as soon as he could. As our life together unfolded, it wasn't always sugarplums and daisies, though we've also had many amazing and happy times. We've had to cling tight to each other to survive 40 years and persevere through the tough times. What we've been through will make you cringe and the hairs on the back of your neck prickle.

> You are extraordinary, and it all starts from within.

During my son's senior year, he stopped putting forward any effort to graduate with his class. It was a battle for him to finish, and he finally graduated later that summer. This was unusual behavior for Rick, because all his life he'd been a happy, energetic, rambunctious, smart kid who loved school. After graduation, he moved out to live with friends, but they soon brought him home because he was acting weird, talking to himself, and saying the TV was sending him private messages.

This was our introduction to the horrific disease of paranoid schizophrenia. It came from nowhere but soon overtook our lives. Our son crumbled before our eyes, turning into an unknown creature, a total stranger. People called Rick insane, crazy, and a lunatic—never just an extremely ill human being. His disease led to five involuntary hospitalizations, psychiatric doctor visits, mandatory medications, and even being hauled off to jail in handcuffs.

The National Alliance on Mental Illness (NAMI) offers free classes to learn about paranoid schizophrenia, and we were glad to take advantage of them. We learned the disease is a lifelong illness with no cure. We learned about the delusions, hallucinations, distinctive movements, and many other odd things unique to this horrible disease. We learned he would have few friends if any, and that he might be unemployable. We learned Rick's whole quality of life rested in our hands as his caregivers, and we'd be responsible for his money, food, and housing.

My desire is for as many families as possible to get relief through NAMI just as I did, so for every copy of this book that's sold, I'm donating $1 directly to NAMI to help them continue to offer love and support to all who need it.

If you're willing to go further to help other humans understand or take better care of a family member with a mental illness, buy my book and promote it on your social media platforms. You can help save someone's child, sibling, parent, or friend from being thrown out into the streets because the families don't understand these difficult people are critically ill humans in crisis.

Unfortunately, Rick's illness wasn't the only cause of our pain. One night I was driving down a dark curvy road on my way home. Suddenly I strained to see something that seemed to be in the middle of the road, and *bam,* there was a bump. My heart started racing, and I asked my son, "What was that?"

He didn't know either, so I did a U-turn and went back to look at what I hit. *Omigod!* It was a person. My brain swirled, my palms sweated on the steering wheel, the hairs on my neck stood straight up. I thought, *Do I go to the corner store to call the police, or do I go home?* It was about the same distance, so I rushed home and screamed for Benny to wake up and come back with me in case they took me to jail. I called the police and returned to the site of the accident.

When I got back to the scene, though the street was blocked off by five sheriff's cars, they let me through. The deputies told me I had run over a woman, and four other cars also ran over her. She was dead. My whole body started shaking violently, and I felt something cold as ice slide down my back.

The deputies asked me over and over what happened. Each time I repeated, "I was driving around the dark curve and suddenly I saw something in the middle of the road and felt the bump. We heard no noise of any kind."

It seemed like an eternity for the investigation to take place, and we couldn't leave until it was completed. After three hours, they let us know she had been released from a nearby jail that morning, and she'd been roaming around the premises and would not leave. She was mentally ill, with no family, and had nowhere to go. They said she wanted to die and this was her suicide plan.

Her death generated a raging storm of guilt, and it consumed most of my mind, energy, and life. Quite a bit of time passed before I could eliminate the voice that kept creeping back in my mind, telling me I had killed someone. I battled post-traumatic stress for a long time.

At the same time, we were struggling financially. Benny had recently bought a $45,000 dump truck. Three weeks after my accident, a driver ran a stop sign and headed right at my husband. Though he did his best to avoid the car, his truck was hit, and he lost control and rolled over, leaving him hanging upside down in his safety belt until help came. Our new dump truck was totaled, and the driver who ran the stop sign died. Benny couldn't work for two months until everything was settled. Our finances went so far in the hole, we had to file bankruptcy.

Since that low point, we've recovered so well we are now debt-free with a credit score of over 800 and assets worth a quarter of a million dollars. I vowed not to allow my past failures, limiting beliefs, or bad circumstances to control me. I learned not to give my power away. We spend only what we have the cash for, we stick to our budget, and we save for a rainy day.

I didn't learn it easily because the past failures and bad circumstances had their hold on us. For years, my family had an unending series of traumas and problems. My dad died very suddenly and unexpectedly when he was only 64. It was painful and shocking to my whole family, and from that time, I helped take care of my mom until her death many years later.

My daughter was married at 18—her decision and most definitely *not* my wish, but I made sure Monica had a beautiful wedding. Twenty years later, with a teen and two pre-teens, she divorced. Their dad then took the children away to live with him, and my daughter left our congregation, which made us very sad. I am so proud of how well our grandchildren have managed their stressful situations.

That's just the beginning of our problems and distractions. My brother is an alcoholic and panhandles to survive. My sister had a 10-pound tumor removed, and I took care of her for a long time as she recovered. Later, she—along with her diabetes, high blood pressure, and painful arthritis—permanently moved in with my husband and me.

My son's illness was finally under control and it ran smoothly for a while, then his psychiatrist decided to change his meds. Rick deteriorated quickly. He talked to the voices that only he could hear in his head. He sat staring into space for hours at a time without moving. He didn't sleep.

My husband Benny works nights, so he wasn't home at 7 a.m. the day a screeching smoke alarm woke me up. I jumped out of bed, scrambled for my shoes, and saw smoke coming out of the vent. First, I went into the bathroom, and there was thick smoke everywhere. Then I panicked, opened the bedroom door, and saw dark smoke pouring out of every vent in the house.

I hollered *"Rick!"* No answer. I ran to his room, grabbed the knob—*it was hot!* I swung the door open and fire came shooting out. The room was pitch black and I couldn't see anything. I kept screaming Rick's name but there was no sound but the crackling of the fire. I was scared, alone, and didn't know if he was in the room or not. The house seemed ready to explode.

Having no cell phone, I ran to get my purse and the cordless phone and went outside to call 9-1-1. We live on 10 acres and the driveway to the street is a quarter of a mile long. My neighbor came into the yard and said he'd seen Rick run down the driveway. I felt relief for at least I knew he wasn't burning to death. I called my husband to come home immediately and my daughter to let her know what was happening. I paced back and forth, praying until the firefighters arrived.

Can you imagine the anguish of not knowing if your son was all right? The sheriff's deputies looked for Rick for two hours before they finally found him, then he was brought to the hospital because he's a diabetic and they wanted to make sure he wasn't dehydrated.

We didn't have a stable place to stay while our house was being repaired, and we were forced to move three times in three months before it was ready for us to return home. It's hard to find a landlord who'll rent to a family with an obviously mentally ill member, much less one who is an arsonist. The state pressed charges, so now my son has a felony arson charge on his record. He ended up at the state hospital for a year and yes, he came home to live with us. Many families won't tolerate their loved ones' mental illness, which is one of the reasons there are so many schizophrenics living on the streets.

Crisis, misfortune, and overpowering circumstances can jolt you into a world where you wonder if life is really worth living. After the fire, I fell apart internally. I was still doing my best to recover when another round of drama befell us. Benny told me his doctor wanted to see us both. We anxiously went to the office, and his doctor bluntly said, "You have cancer."

We turned and looked at each other as a chill went down my spine and my whole body began to shake. We sat there, numb, not knowing what to do, say, think, ask. We wondered, *do we cry, scream, panic? Now what?* The doctor calmly recommended surgery because Benny is young. He didn't want the tumors to ruthlessly spread from organ to organ and into his bones, squeezing life from his body. We agreed to surgery.

After surgery, my husband recovered well. His checkups were clean, but I was in so much psychological pain from the emotional roller coaster I'd been riding that I couldn't move forward. That was when we were introduced to a type of coffee with a special ingredient to help support the immune system. To my amazement, it transformed me, and I quickly began to feel happy and content.

I'd never dreamed I'd feel so good again. Benny found it enhanced his quality of life, too. Eight of our family members now drink it as well and we all feel we live and feel better. I list the URL for Organo Gold in my contact information, and I urge you to try some if you too are stressed.

Six years after Benny's surgery, the dreaded day arrived: Cancer showed its ugly head again. This time, the recommendation was 40 radiation treatments, and he's still in the process of taking them. Our spiritual family has been overwhelmingly loving and supportive as members of our congregation take turns preparing and delivering a hot meal to our doorstep. Every day, a member of our congregation picks up Benny, takes him for his treatment, waits in the car, and brings him home. We are so relieved we aren't going through this challenge alone.

We have researched how to improve the odds of a good outcome, and we discovered seed-based nutrition, which we've added to our diets. I've included the URL for Rain in my contact information because I am certain Rain is why Benny can continue to work 12-hour days with minimal side effects as he goes through his radiation treatment. I've also replaced pesky toxins that were lurking and hiding in our home with Modere products; the URL for those also is included in my contact information.

I know by now you're wondering *how does this lady remain sane?* In the past, I felt as though I would die from all the anguish each time my heart shattered into a million pieces. It's been a heck of a wild ride.

At the beginning of this chapter, I mentioned the bitter pill I swallowed that made me believe I didn't deserve much from life and would always have the short end of the stick. The side effects of that pill shackled me for years as I went through the motions of living and pretty much just waited to die.

Now I wholly believe God does not give me more than I can bear, and that is what gives me the courage to wait for the time when He will end all suffering here on earth.

Now I pray often and read biblical accounts of how others have suffered tremendously. I'm encouraged by how God lavishly blessed them in overabundance as long as they remained faithful to him, no matter how disastrous their circumstances.

It is only through the grace of God that I courageously keep my chin up and stand *tall* to reach my golden moment. I'm eternally grateful to be healing from emotional trauma, and I long to do something for the world. I practice gratitude because I cannot be grateful and sad simultaneously. No, it is not easy, but now I can smile and have a zest for life, and my loving and supportive husband stands by my side.

Hey, look how *far* I've come!

I challenge you to get over the belief that old age means it's too late to change. If you can breathe, age doesn't matter at all in your plans to have a grand life. Life is 10% what happens to you and 90% how you react to it. Your setbacks could be *your* setup for greatness.

Stand *tall*!

# Author's Notes

I was born in Austin, Texas where I've spent most of my life, and where my husband, Benny, and I live now. As an entrepreneur with several businesses, I have the freedom to work from home. Benny and I have two children, Monica and Rick, and three wonderful grandchildren, Josue, Caleb, and Franki.

Please check out my websites to find out more about my businesses; I offer you many opportunities to grow healthier and to save money while you do so. Contact me for a free code to save money on travel, seed nutrition, coffee, nutraceuticals, and toxin-free household products.

I look forward to helping and working with you.

# Contact Information

**Email:** 1dcmacias@gmail.com
**Facebook:** Dolores Macias (Casarez)
**Websites:** www.dcmacias.myibuumerang.com
www.dcmacias.OrganoGold.com
www.rainintl.com/dcmacias
www.Modere.com/5446915

Chapter 10

# What Brings You Joy?

### Gabriel Retana

When I was a child growing up in Costa Rica, I loved horses and cows and just wanted to be a farmer like my grandfather. My family moved to the United States when I was eight to pursue a more prosperous future, and something changed in me. I started dreaming of success.

At first, I naturally wanted success to come as a side effect of my passion and skill. I knew I wanted to master something because I have always admired masters of their craft, whether they're in sports, business, or manual labor. It is fascinating to watch a master at work.

At some point, my signals got crossed. Success began to become the end result in itself, not how I was getting there. When someone fantasizes or dreams of becoming successful too long, their dream is of the spoils of that success—what they'll get, how wealthy they will become, and how it will feel to have finally "made it."

That is impure.

The secret of other-worldly success is purity, sincerity, and authenticity.

When you act impurely, you never have your full faculties at your command. You are always distracted by the pleasure of the outcome. Chasing pleasure, chasing the fringe benefits of success, effectively handcuffs you. Therefore, the real-world consequence of impurity is ineffectiveness.

I became an over-achiever and perfectionist. Much of my life was transient, and I didn't put down roots. My family moved a lot, and I met new people and started over most years, attending nine different schools before I graduated from high school.

> *A life worth living is a life in which the chase for happiness comes to an end.*

I chose to attend The University of North Carolina at Chapel Hill, not because it was the most prestigious, but because my intuition told me it was the place where I'd grow the most as a person. But I still deviated from sincerity and was looking for a major that would set me up for the most success in life instead of studying something I actually enjoyed. When I changed my major to Exercise and Sports Science, my academic performance dramatically improved and I was happier and more at peace.

After I graduated, I moved to Miami and joined Teach for America, planning to go to medical school in a few years. Fresh out of college, I was teaching seven periods of biology to kids at a failing school, coaching football, acting as the team's strength and conditioning coach, taking organic chemistry online, and helping the local chapter of La Unidad Latina, Lambda Upsilon Lambda Fraternity Inc. as the Line Dean for their new member intakes. My pattern of being an overachiever and perfectionist continued, and I burned out quickly.

I was toast and ready to quit before Thanksgiving. But I pushed on. And pushed. I'm not a quitter. I had a two-year commitment to teach. My promise and my integrity are everything to me. I survived weekend to weekend, holiday to holiday.

I was completely overwhelmed in the spring, and I knew for the sake of my health I needed to step away and take care of myself. I couldn't even make it to the end of the year. How pathetic is that? But I had hit a tipping point of unwellness. Mentally, physically, and emotionally, I was screwed up.

A friend of mine recruited me to a travel club network marketing business, and I thought, "Worst case, I'll go on some awesome vacations and explore the world. Best case, I create financial freedom for me and my loved ones." During the next six years, I went on more than 100 trips and vacations. Personal development became a daily part of my life, and I became a personal development junkie.

Up to that point, I'd never really known what I wanted to do in life, other than make a lot of money and help a lot of people. I wanted to learn how to help people create *true* wealth. Not some flash in the pan gimmick. *True* abundance.

After six years of an up and down business, it was time to do a self-evaluation. I realized I wasn't making the kind of money I'd hoped for, and neither was my team. It was time for something else.

So I went to a Les Brown event where Johnny Wimbrey also spoke. The event's format was gurus pitching you their programs: real estate investing, options trading, becoming a guru yourself and writing a book, making money on Amazon, making money on eBay, etc. After the presentations, I met Johnny in the back of the room and I asked him for some advice.

"Johnny, I'm interested in *everything*, so how do I choose what to do?"

*You can't go after everything or you won't get anything.* These may not have been Johnny's exact words, but they're close enough. They made sense then and they still do. I took his advice and didn't sign up for the six courses I wanted. Instead, I picked just one: investing in real estate. I had heard most first-time millionaires make their money in real estate.

Now I needed a new hobby, and I found Brazilian jiu-jitsu. I applied my knowledge of kinesiology, biomechanics, and the human body to intense training in BJJ. I figured becoming a black belt in the most distinguished martial art in the world would be life-changing. Besides, I missed the challenge of a high-level sport.

I quickly fell in love with the art. I didn't do it to win medals, or to become healthy, or to be able to kick someone's ass. It was my lab. I got a chance to test every nugget of personal development that I'd absorbed. I started to understand the concepts all those greats have known.

I share these concepts with my students, and I will share them with you. It's a humble thing to ask how you can improve incrementally. But the consequences of maintained incremental improvement are anything but modestly incremental. You get compound interest in incremental improvement.

*The rich get richer and the poor get poorer* is a famous old saying known as The Matthew Effect, and it comes from the book of Matthew:

*For to everyone who has, more will be given, and he will have abundance; but from him who does not have, even what he has will be taken away.*
**—Matthew 12:29, New King James Version**

While it's a harsh concept, it's actually an effective description of the way the world works, and there's a reason for that. A very solid, scientific reason: When you start to wander off the path, the probability that you will wander further off the path increases exponentially.

That is the concept of hell. But as you improve, the probability that each improvement will produce a further improvement increases. Perhaps the downside is the cataclysmic catastrophe that you can engage upon if your bad habits run you. The upside is that each improvement produces an increment in the probability of the next improvement.

All self-help can be broken down into simple steps. First, establish your aim. What is your burning desire? Next, break down your goal into attainable units.

Eliminate resistance, and then just let it rip. Go after it with everything you got.

Your positive consequences reward and reinforce you every time you manage an accomplishment:

Your character becomes a little stronger

You gain a little more confidence in your ability

You become a little less racked with self-disgust

You grow a little more hopeful about the future

You become more certain you can make another positive change

Reward yourself for your incremental improvements. Don't chase pleasure or achievements for their sakes. Be patient, don't get too cynical, and think, "Okay, just imagine what might happen if I keep doing this every week for 10 years."

In reality, you can't really begin to imagine the scope of the improvements you'll make and how much better things will be for you if you keep on that path, even just some of the time.

The most important part to really grasp is this:

*A master is one who focuses on ever-finer detail and refines the action until achievement.*

That's a very good way of progressing with your life. You won't become a master of your mind and body unless you know what is at the core of driving all your actions.

When you do something because the thing *itself* drives you, its purity—not the fringe benefits or the door prize—then you gain all the faculties you need. All your talents become available to you.

If you are reading this book, most likely you have at least dipped your toe into personal growth and development. This isn't new stuff. Ask and you shall receive, seek and you shall find, think and grow rich, thoughts become things. That is fundamental.

You may have thought, *If I believe I'm the one, my power comes from within. I believe in myself, so what am I waiting for?*

So, why *are* you procrastinating? Why hasn't your goal manifested?

If this is the case, your level of sincerity and seriousness has not reached a fever pitch. In my case, my real accomplishments only happen when I am *all in*.

*But burning desire can burn you.*

So, if the burning desire is so powerful it can deliver anything you want, is there a downside? There can be.

Desire is a contract you make with yourself to be unhappy until you get what you want. You start becoming disturbed because you want something, and then you work hard to get it and you are miserable in the meantime. Unfortunately, when you finally get what you desired, you don't get to stay in that blissful moment, enjoying your victory. At that moment, you revert to the state you were in before you got it.

How can you avoid getting burned by your own desire?

Remaining detached from the outcome while you pursue your goal is your key to inner peace. The pursuit of success is almost always spurred by a fear of failure. Behind every success, there is always great insecurity, the insecurity of wondering *Will I make it?*

And that insecurity, that fear of failure, actually leads to flailing around and increases the odds you *won't* make it. I've been at that point so many times in my life.

You turn into a hard-working drone, beating yourself to the bone and filled with fantastical ideas that are driven by fear and anxiety.

When we're riddled with doubt, frustration, and impatience—all just figments of our imagination—we're just reacting to and projecting our fears. When we identify with any of these three emotions, we just create more of the same on the journey.

When you're able to keep your anxiety and fear of not making your goal at bay, then the quality of your efforts improves drastically. When *I won't make it* is no longer part of your mindset or language, your entire life and journey improve.

Even better, if you manage to believe *I will make it*, your choices and actions will be drastically different and more effective than when you're spurred by the anxiety and fear of possibly *not* making it.

Where there is purity and a lack of fear in your actions, where you have a sense of doing something in a very focused way for a very focused outcome, you'll begin to feel in your heart that your goal is accessible.

Purity is not a rule—it's not better, or more correct, it's simply more effective. It's just a way to do things that results in the least interference. It's a way to approach goals with all your faculties and talents in your back pocket.

*To be worried or concerned about the manner of their unfoldment is to hold these fertile seeds in a mental grasp and, therefore, to prevent them from really maturing to full harvest.*

— **Neville Goddard.**

We maintain a fantasy that there's something out there that will make us happy and fulfilled forever. That's a complete delusion. No one thing can do that. Rather, it's a *process*—of understanding, self-discovery, training yourself, and seeing certain truths. Happiness is just returning to a state of being where nothing is missing and you have no burning desires.

A life worth living is a life in which the chase for happiness comes to an end.

In my case, I could never have predicted my life's path. I found a way to put the full spectrum of my gifts, skills, passions, and interests together when I founded GROW Academy, an educational company providing wealth and wellness coaching, mentorship, and seminars. At GROW, we teach people to take back control of their mind, body, and wealth. I use all movement arts—yoga, mobility, calisthenics, and martial arts—to help people explore the various ways they can grow and contribute, and seek truth, understanding, and inner peace.

Brazilian jiu-jitsu is a journey of truth-seeking. The majority of my work as a coach and instructor is helping students remove their hang-ups and false ideas, both mental and physical. I cultivate an environment for them to grow, to fall in love with the art. It's not my job to change my students or help them improve. They have everything within themselves.

This story was very helpful while I was trying to let go of inner resistance, and I share it often:

Once upon a time, there was a Chinese farmer whose horse ran away. That evening, all of his neighbors came around to commiserate. They said, "We are so sorry to hear your horse has run away. This is most unfortunate."

The farmer said, "Maybe."

The next day the horse came back bringing seven wild horses with it, and in the evening everybody came back and said, "Oh, isn't that lucky. What a great turn of events. You now have eight horses!"

The farmer again said, "Maybe."

The following day, his son tried to break one of the horses. While riding, he was thrown and broke his leg. The neighbors then said, "Oh dear, that's too bad."

The farmer responded, "Maybe."

The next day, the conscription officers came around to conscript people into the army, and they rejected his son because of his broken leg. Again all the neighbors came around and exclaimed, "Isn't that great!"

Again, the farmer said only, "Maybe."

Take a moment to reflect on this story. All too often we automatically label an experience *bad* if we hate it, and *good* if we like it. Remember the bad cannot exist without the good, and vice versa. Whatever experience happens in our life, we can never be sure of the consequences it may bring to our future.

You don't need to look back or even into the future. Where are you *right now*? What makes you tick? What gets you excited in the morning about living another day? What brings you joy?

Before you can spread joy, you must have it. To impart delight, you need to be somewhat delightful. And to be delightful is not some trick of making yourself look delightful. When you're doing things that are delightful to you, you become delightful to others. The secret of success is making what you're doing interesting to others.

Be interested yourself, and others will find you interesting. Arm yourself with specific knowledge, which you find by pursuing your innate talents, genuine curiosity, and passion. You don't find it by going to school for whatever is the hottest job or going into whatever field investors say is the hottest. The most interesting things cannot be taught, but everything can be learned.

Find, build, or create something that looks like work to others but feels like play to you. Clients, customers, and partners will find you and pay you handsomely for your services.

When you find inner peace, you'll also gain great strength. The person who has found inner peace can no longer be intimidated, controlled, manipulated, or programmed. In this state, we are invulnerable to the threats of the world and have, therefore, mastered earthly life.

# Author's Notes

My work in real estate has given me a deep understanding of wealth and what it means to have true financial freedom. Comprehending the laws of nature, the mind, and the human body and its movement have been my life obsessions. For 15 years, I have been pouring my resources into my

life project, GROW Academy (Gabriel Retana Organization Worldwide). GROW Academy's mission is to help those who are willing to be serious seize control of their freedom in multiple dimensions: Freedom of their mind, of their movements, and their finances.

It brings me great joy to see my clients shatter the shackles of financial slavery that have cursed them, to see them move in ways they never imagined possible, and to see them reach inner peace. All of the money I make from my business I reinvest back into education, research, and infrastructure to serve my clients better. We will build wellness retreats around the world.

Because I also love learning as well as teaching, I train Brazilian Jiu-Jitsu under Zach Davis at the Fort Martial Arts Academy and mixed-movement arts under Budokon founder Cameron Shayne. I am also a project manager at our family-run painting business, Retana Painting, and Wallcoverings, the top painting business in the D.C.-Maryland-Virginia metro area.

## Contact Information

**Email:** Gabriel@GabrielRetana.com
**Websites:** GabrielRetana.com
**Facebook:** gabrielretana2
**Instagram:** @gabrielretana
**YouTube:** Gabriel Retana

# Chapter 11

# Live Life *On* Purpose, And *With* Purpose

### Yolanda Jones

At some point in our lives, we all need to answer a powerful and life-changing question: *Why am I here?*

Our journey to answer this overarching question begins the moment we become aware there's more to life than just our mundane daily activities. Our awareness triggers a greater internal awakening, one that won't let us rest until the purpose behind our existence is discovered.

The day we finally collide with our destiny is the day the entire trajectory of our life shifts, and we realize the foundation for our existence supersedes us. Our search has always been greater than just learning about ourselves. Instead, it's about our ability to serve others in a way that allows us to impact our lives for eternity. You see, I believe we were created on purpose, because I believe nothing in the world *just happens*. We were put here for a specific reason, to reach a select audience, and only we can fulfill this calling.

Now, let's look specifically at *you*. You were created *with a purpose*. You have unique gifts, talents, skills, and creativity within you, specific to you alone. When you use these God-given characteristics to serve others well, you leave a lasting impression on the hearts of others and make your imprint in the world. With great resilience, you are proudly able to stand and say, *This is what I was put on earth to do.*

> Allow God to orchestrate the plan that He has for your life.

Hello, new you, for your life has truly just begun! Your number-one goal should be to live out your life knowing you were put here for a purpose, searching and not stopping until you find out what that purpose is. Yes, friends, your life has purpose, and it is your quest to find it, embrace it, embark upon it, and give birth to all God has placed inside of you as you rise up and live purposefully.

Living your life purposefully takes a lot of courage and inner strength. It's one thing to just tap into the higher calling God has planned for your life. However, it's an entirely different reality when you're confronted with *how* you are to bring said greatness into fruition.

You can only manifest this high-level destiny by maintaining the right mindset. First, you *must* believe your being here is not an accident, that you're not simply existing. You need to believe you were placed on earth to specifically serve as an answer to someone else's problem, someone who's living in a downtrodden world.

You were designed to shed light and love on everyone you encounter at all times. You're meant to flow at high vibrations, friend, as your life creates something of such high magnitude that it'll far outlive your very existence. The beauty in all of this is that no one can surpass you at being *you*. Only *you* have the power to show up as your authentic self. Only you, with grace and fortitude, can leave others in far better condition than when you found them, and perhaps forever transformed.

Indeed, *purpose* requires having the right frame of mind to elevate yourself to the top level and announce to the world, *This is my time, so why not me!* I truly believe you can accomplish anything you attempt. A life far greater than you have ever imagined exists—without a doubt. First, though, you must create the world for your new life, using the limitless imagination with which we all are endowed. You must become fully aware you were created for more—*for excellence!*—and you must not become content until you're deep into the purpose-driven life created for you before you were even in the womb.

For all of us, though, reaching the world we were meant for begins with the stories we tell ourselves, with what we believe to be true. Self-sabotage can be our most debilitating act. If we are going to take our calling to the next level, we must master the mental directives that govern our ability to become the best version of ourselves. As we begin to take control of our thoughts and weigh them with truth, we must believe with all of our hearts that there is purpose for our existence, and we have a mandate to follow these instructions. Our instructions were given to us on purpose, for a specific purpose, and we are called to live our purpose with due diligence.

I am convinced many of us have not tapped into our God-given purpose because we haven't been able to grasp its scope and capture it within our minds. If we're not able to envision *more*, we will never be able to attract the abundance we desire and deserve. Often, what holds us back is just the willingness to make a simple mental shift to assess where we are in life.

Perhaps no one else has told you about the power of your mind. Let me be the first to encourage you to take the initiative to dig deep within, daily, to discover your purpose from the inside out. Your mind is your most powerful weapon. Allow it to be the fuel you need to live each day unapologetically, and with purpose!

As we spend quiet time looking within—whether it's prayer, meditation, dreaming, spending time in nature, or just *being*—we'll gain an understanding of the options offered by our Creator. Those quiet times let us tap into a world that is infinitely bigger and better than where we are.

Once we realize we want more, we're propelled onto a new path, a new world. It truly does exist. You, my friend, are indeed created to become more than you are at this very moment. That in itself is worth getting excited about!

**The Transformation.** Once your mind accepts and is in alignment with the belief you were created *on* purpose and *with* a purpose, changes immediately take place in you, from the inside out. You begin to see the world around you differently, and you're no longer satisfied with the mediocre lifestyle you once admired. This is when you begin to function at a higher capacity than you ever knew existed. You'll have found your *why*.

Let me warn you to be vigilant, though. As you're transformed, your old belief system will rear its ugly head and do its best to encourage you to passively drift back into the older, lesser version of yourself, the one that didn't serve your purpose and kept you trapped in mediocrity. You must be intentional in how you show up every single day and work on yourself.

Let's unpack this a little deeper.

The factor I have found that is most essential in maintaining a healthy mindset for a purposeful life is what we feed ourselves daily. Let me explain. The messages absorbed via channels such as social media, television, podcasts, news, and even the conversations we have with others, greatly impact what we think about and what we keep in our minds. The constant often negative chatter counteracts what we know to be true and most excellent for our lives.

Let's go even deeper, shall we? Let's say I listen to a podcast on implementing a daily routine of speaking affirmations first thing in the morning. If I choose to apply those healthy routines every day with the goal of building myself a more positive character, these beneficial thoughts and actions will seep into my subconscious. By default, they become part of my way of life, and they allow me to go out and live more purposefully, simply because I've changed the way I see myself and the world around me.

This equally applies to negative input we allow to fill our thoughts and feed our minds. When I watch and listen to hopeless or hurtful news, shows, and people, my subconscious becomes tainted with negativity, and I can lose my desire for *more*. The lack of this purpose will make me more passive, less willing to better myself via life-long learning. I'll be less likely to go out and help change the lives of others, and I probably won't be walking in the purpose for which I've been ordained.

Both outcomes clearly result from the quality of what we feed our minds and our subconscious. We must not allow our purpose to be diminished by feeding on thoughts that are less than God's best for our existence here on earth. By building ourselves up, we can be, do and have *all* that has been made available to us. There are no limits once we discover our *why* and embrace it.

As you are being converted into the powerhouse you were designed to be, the people with whom you surround yourself will greatly influence your purpose. I sincerely believe it can be very challenging (if not impossible) to grow into your calling while you're surrounded by people who don't encourage and support you as you become great. They can easily kill your dreams.

Here's a bit of wisdom to remember: You are the average of the five people who surround you. Stay aware of the company you keep and the quality of what they're feeding your mind. Be ruthless if necessary. You may need to weed out some "friends" so you can stay on your journey to greatness and living life *on* purpose, and *with* purpose.

Unfortunately, it may also mean you decide to spend less time with family members who, with the best of intentions, hold you back. Often, it's just due to their limited knowledge of what you've been summoned to accomplish which brings up a point I need to emphasize as you commit to your transformation to a more fruitful life: *Living purposefully takes sacrifice.* Indeed, the path to greatness is costly, and it's worth every bit of what you invest into transitioning into someone who is priceless in comparison.

It's not easy to change from passively living a life where you're just getting by to purposefully living a life that is overflowing with excellence and abundance. A successful transition calls for you to invest in yourself in order to advance. You will have to enroll in courses, attend conferences, and perhaps even travel to be exposed to greater thinking. You will soak in knowledge from those who have already gone down the path you're currently traveling. You'll sometimes have to get out of your comfort zone in order to achieve a purpose-filled life.

Growing often feels uncomfortable, but it's always necessary before you can reach your next level. The amazing thing about living a life of purpose is that you may not always feel qualified to do what you're directed to do. Don't try to put all of the pieces together yourself. Allow God to orchestrate the plan He has for your life. He will, with great intentionality and strategy, morph your life into the great masterpiece He had in mind for you all along.

The process of growing may also call for you to give up some favorite things. For example, you will probably need to spend fewer hours watching your favorite TV shows or hanging out with friends. Instead, you'll invest your time in more fruitful activities, ones that will yield a better return on investment as they help you fulfill your destiny. You must spend time with individuals who add value to your calling. The goal is to be propelled, not derailed, from the original plan which was designed for you.

You may have to change the way you've always done things if you are committed to seeing your life grow and flourish. Even though you grew up with certain principles or guidelines by which you previously governed your life, be willing to pivot when necessary so you can make the effort to take on higher ground for God's kingdom.

Change is inevitable, and critical, to live a life flooded with destiny. Stay open to the vast possibilities of what can be produced when you are willing to cleave to new ideas. If you are going to live a transformed life filled with purpose, you must be willing to put in the work so you can live it well.

**More.** As you reflect on where you are, allow me to encourage you to go for more. There are more opportunities, more ground to cover, more ways you should show up serving others, more knowledge to attain, and more impact you should be making.

Living your life purposefully does not require you to be a skilled imitator of someone else. It is simply a matter of showing up and being your authentic self. Everything you need to be a game-changer was already placed within you at birth. It is now time to rise up and spread all of the amazing, unique seeds that are already inside of you. Allow those seeds to germinate and blossom into the beauty you were designed for so all the world can see. There can be no more thinking small or accepting less than God's best for your life. Let's go out and live a life *on* purpose and *with* purpose!

# Author's Notes

I am a compassionate educator, aspiring professional speaker, and life coach. My greatest passion is to serve others, whether through teaching, volunteering, or naturally building relationships. As I help others achieve their dreams, seeing their *aha!* light-bulb moments never get old.

As a life-long learner, I am intentional in growing and investing in myself, and my number-one goal is to motivate others to do the same. I work to influence others to become more than they ever knew was possible, be confident in who they are, while they embrace the person they are becoming, and achieve all that life has to offer.

Growing up and living my entire life in Dallas, I'm the youngest of six children, and blessed to still have my mother as an active part of my life. She's been my rock and my biggest cheerleader ever since I can remember. I am a graduate of Dallas Baptist University, where I majored in English as a Second Language (ESL) and earned my master's degree in Liberal Arts.

I am also the proud mother of a beautiful daughter, Jazmin. My hobbies include traveling, sightseeing and going on new adventures, reading, watching comedy/suspense movies, and spending time with family and friends. I always find time to serve others in my church and community via volunteer opportunities.

Life is an adventure, and I unapologetically plan to enjoy every moment of the journey I am blessed to embark upon.

## Contact Information

**Email:** yolandajallen2012@gmail.com
**Facebook:** Yolanda Jones Allen
**Instagram:** Yolanda Jones Allen

# Chapter 12

# What Are You *Feeling*?

### David Peacock

> *Whatever the mind of man can conceive and believe, it can achieve.*
> —**Napoleon Hill.**

As a species, we truly underestimate the power of our minds. My objective is to help you to gain a better understanding of how your mind operates so you can experience mental wealth—*right here, right now.*

On a separate piece of paper, please write: "A crystal-clear picture plus how a heightened sense of feeling affects your external world." Now write your definition of this statement as you think it applies to you. We'll get back to this exercise later, and I'll explain why I've asked you to do this.

When we analyze people active in personal development, we identify two general types. First, those who take action and do what they are told to do, whether it's by books, podcasts, videos, audios, or their mentors, get great results. Then, there are those who study (and study) and take no action. When they don't see results, they question what they are learning and allow their external environment to reinforce their doubts, all because they don't know how to analyze the results they are getting.

> *You can't control anything outside you, but what you can control is yourself.*

Let's be honest with each other. At the beginning of this chapter, I asked you to write a statement down on a separate piece of paper and define it. Did you do so?

I will share my firsthand experience. For almost two years, I studied, took little action, and got very few positive results. When I was 28, I told my father I would be a millionaire by the time I was thirty. When my 30th birthday came around and I had no more money then I had before, it was even more embarrassing because I had all of this knowledge and no results to show for it.

I now know that once we *apply* what we learn, we will experience the desired result. You could read this book and a thousand more, or you could do what the other authors and I suggest in this book—**apply what you learn!**

You're probably thinking, "Who *is* this guy to make a statement like that?" But if you apply one or two of the ideas in my chapter alone, not to mention the ideas from the other brilliant people in this book, *I guarantee you* your life will change.

At the end of this chapter, I will give you three action steps that can change your life forever. But will you do them? That question is for you to answer.

Our universe operates in a specific way, a way no one can manipulate or change. I am not going to define universal laws, but I can give you an understanding of how these laws influence your life.

Let's start by taking a look at you. Do you believe me when I say that everything is energy? Do you believe me when I say that you, as a human, are a spiritual being living in a physical body?

A human baby is one of the most helpless mammals on the planet, requiring nurturing and constant care for at least the first decade of its life in order to survive. If other species needed this much care, most would be extinct. For example, if a newborn gazelle can't run fast, the next lion that comes by will eat it.

When you arrived on planet earth, you absorbed all the energy that your parents, guardians, and environment provided, however well-done, misguided, or cockeyed their parenting might be. You took their energies and accepted them as your own because you didn't know differently.

Fast forward to today, and you're living with the beliefs you were taught and inherited—and they apply to every aspect of your life.

My parents are hard-working, loving people, the same with my grandparents, and I am sure my great-grandparents, as well. Growing up, I never had to worry about food being on the table or not being able to play sports. My younger brother and I had wonderful childhoods. My family has a cottage off the coast of Vancouver, and we spent every summer there. As children, we had total freedom, playing flashlight tag, going on adventures, boating, and dirt biking. It was an amazing place to grow up, and I grew up not having to worry about anything.

My point is that we accept all the beliefs our environment provides us

All our parents did the best they could do based on what they knew. You might disagree, saying, "That's a load of crap; my family wasn't there for me." Or perhaps, "My parents abused me in so many ways." But, think—what environment did *they* grow up in? It was probably very similar to what you experienced, so again, they did the best they could with what they knew.

While you didn't choose your conditioning, let's make it very clear that no one else has the responsibility to change it. It's *your* responsibility. If you want to blame others, you have a losing mentality. If you don't like your results, you need to change them. If you *feel* a certain way, that's on you.

You can't control anything outside you, but what you *can* control is yourself! *Your* thoughts, *your feelings*, *your* actions. It's time to realize that. That is the life you were given, so make the best out of it.

What I've written will not resonate with all readers. That's not my job. It will resonate with some of you, though, and if it helps shift the course of one of you, then writing this chapter was worth it.

For most of my life, I felt as though I didn't belong, like I was in a foreign land, being looked at like an alien. (Some would refer to the *feeling* as being a Starseed; Google the term if you haven't heard it.) When I spoke, somehow others didn't hear or understand the way I explained my thoughts. Often the *feelings* I had were tough to explain. This was difficult for me because I still didn't know who I was, so I was constantly looking for justification and approval from the outside.

As I grew older, I tried to suppress my "differentness." I put tremendous pressure on myself, doing things that everyone else wanted me to be doing, trying to live up to others' expectations. Like going to college—what a joke that was. I didn't want to go, but I did because everyone else said I should. I lasted one semester. When my dad asked about my grades, I'd lie, saying "Oh, they don't give grades." Later, the family joke was that I was just going to matinees. The pathetic truth was that I did go to all my classes, but I didn't do any of the homework and I flunked all the tests and assignments. I was taking business, administration, and finance. Let's just say that those classes were not my cup of tea.

Once I wasn't going to my "matinees" anymore, I needed to work, and I had a number of jobs. One job was as a curbside recycler where I picked up recycling from the blue bins in front of houses. When I turned 22, still working full time as a recycler, I tried my luck at real estate on the side and sold one house in two years. That ended pretty abruptly.

From there, I went on to work for a family friend; he gave me a great role in his company and lots of opportunities. I stayed with him for just over four years, but I didn't *feel* fulfilled. I felt like I was just existing. During that time, I was also going through the process of becoming a firefighter, something I believed I would enjoy.

In September 2017, I went to a good friend's really spectacular wedding, and when it was over, a few of us wanted to keep the party going. I suggested a restaurant that employed a girl I found attractive. It turned out she wasn't attracted back, so I sat at the bar and had a serious talk with a friend, back and forth about ways we could earn more money, sharing deep thoughts about if there could be a better way of living this game of life.

While I was brushing my teeth later that night, that same friend sent me a video of mixed martial arts fighter Conor McGregor talking about the law of attraction. (I later thought, ironically, it was the law of attraction that attracted me to the law of attraction.) As I watched the video, I was blown away, "You're telling me, all I have to do is think about what I want, see it on the screen of my mind, create a heightened sense of *feeling*, and *boom*, I can have it?"

As I continued to study the law of attraction, I came across Bob Proctor and our celebrity co-author Les Brown. Everything Bob said resonated with me and made so much sense. I said to myself, "This guy knows something, and I want to work with him." So, I did. I decided to invest in myself and become a *Thinking into Results* consultant.

My friends and family's reaction to my new path and commitment caused me a lot of heartache and confusion. When I told my mom and dad about becoming a mindset coach and how fired up I was, they said almost simultaneously, "You're still going to be a firefighter, right?" It may seem contradictory, but their inability to understand the depth of my commitment confirmed my decision; I knew being a coach is exactly what I wanted and needed.

I want and need to help people develop their awareness about who they are and the potential they possess, help them achieve their goals, and live a life by design.

Without support from the people that I'd hoped would support me, I was completely on my own. It was a tough time, but it was time for me to change in order to make a difference in people's lives. I decided to utilize all the information I had gained over six months and write a book with one of my first clients, a good friend of mine, who is also a talented rapper. We wrote a personal development book, *Awareness: The Groundwork for Fulfillment* and Bob Proctor wrote the foreword.

My mindset was changing so quickly, but the results weren't matching my pace. Sure, I had a book and a few clients, but that big shift wasn't happening for me. It goes to show how strong our conditioning is, and I will touch on that a little later. I was fed up with my environment, and my relationships with my family and friends weren't healthy or supportive. I knew I had to change my environment, so I made the decision to move to Toronto. I packed up everything I could fit in my 2005 Pontiac Sunfire and drove from Vancouver to Toronto with no idea of where I was going to live, just a fresh mind and a desire to succeed.

The most I had ever earned in a year was $50,000, but I was good about saving money and had $100,000 in the bank. I began to invest in myself, and a couple of years later I was almost $40,000 in debt. Though I made these investments in myself, I was still trapped by my old conditioning. Because I was still taking action in ways that weren't conducive to how I was *feeling*, the results were not what I wished. Many of us who are investing in personal development suffer from this inability to recognize how we're enmeshed in our conditioning.

Let's talk about changing our conditioning. The subconscious mind is a powerful tool and it programs how your body works 97% of the time. Your subconscious is driven by the conditioning you've had since you were born, the environment, and parents, as I discussed at the beginning of this chapter. The way to change the subconscious programming is through repetition, changing your point of attraction.

So, let's say you see a motivational video, or you read an inspirational book, and now you have the desire and ambition to earn more money. Sorry, it won't happen until your beliefs change, driving a change in your subconscious conditioning, your programming.

*So, what can I do to change?* you ask.

Do you remember what I said at the beginning of the chapter, about giving you three action steps that will change your life? Here they are.

Changing your conditioning is done through reprogramming, using affirmations, visualization, and meditation. Think back to what I asked you to write earlier, "A crystal-clear picture plus a heightened sense of *feeling* affect your external world."

Look where the power is—97% of the power is in the subconscious. Let's use that 97% for the good of mankind and ourselves. Transfer that power to a new belief in your perception. Get yourself to an elevated state, and transfer that energy using a decision from the conscious mind to channel that energy to focus on what you want. {Note: Have you written the sentence and the definition *yet*?}

***Affirmation.*** When you make an affirmation, you declare to the universe exactly what you want, ideally in a short statement using the present tense.

Here's an example: *I am an inspirational speaker, helping millions of people around the globe develop awareness as to who they are.*

Be clear to yourself about what you affirm. The universe doesn't speak English, it communicates by vibration, so it's about the *feeling* you are projecting when you make an affirmation. Once you create an affirmation, I want you to write it down, say it out loud, and tape it, and listen to it every day! Write it 10 times, say it 10 times, and listen to it on loop for 10 minutes.

***Visualization.*** When you visualize, you create a mental image of what you want. I wrote earlier about having a crystal-clear picture. Whether it's just one still image or a moving picture, include as much energy and *feeling* as you can.

My example builds a mental image of the affirmation above: *I see myself in the present, speaking on stage in front of thousands of people, and imagine how that would make me* feel. *I allow that feeling to enter every cell of my being.*

Do this for 5-10 minutes every day, right before you go to sleep.

***Meditation.*** Meditation helps you clear your brain and emotions, and it allows your mind to visualize easier as well as hear yourself more clearly.

There are many forms of meditation and many ways to get into a meditative state. If you are new to meditation, use a guided meditation; there are plenty to choose from online. The goal behind this is to just *be*, with no thought of anything else. Focus on just one thing, such as your breathing. You will notice your thoughts keep intruding, and when you veer off on side trips, catch yourself and bring your mind back to your breath.

It's like training at the gym; you have to keep exercising your muscles if you want them to improve. In this case, you're exercising your brain. Meditate for a minimum of 15 minutes per day.

I challenge you to do these three exercises every day for 21 days. If you don't complete all three on the same day, you need to start over at day one. It will be easier if you find someone to hold you accountable.

Evaluate the changes in yourself after 21 days. They will depend on how deep your beliefs are as well as how thoroughly you follow my guidelines. Do you agree to continue on this path? I suggest you do—keep going.

I only suggested 21 days because it's easy to commit for such a short time.

Everything you need for change is in this book. Apply what you are learning from the *Power of Mental Wealth* and see what difference it makes in your life.

Enjoy your personal growth and as always . . . keep smiling!

# Author's Notes

I am an elite-level mindset coach, public speaker, professional network marketer, and co-author of *Awareness: The Groundwork for Fulfillment*. I am fully dedicated to helping people develop their awareness of who they are and the potential they possess, achieve their dreams, and live a life by design.

Growing up in Coquitlam, British Columbia, a suburb of Vancouver, I was graduated from Centennial High School and later studied at the Proctor Gallagher Institute. I reside in Toronto and am single.

## Contact Information

**Email:** peacockconsulting10@gmail.com
**Website:** groundworkforfulfillment.com
**Instagram:** @peacockconsulting
**Facebook:** Expand your Mind with David Peacock
**YouTube:** Expand your MIND with David Peacock

## Chapter 13

# Reach For the Stars And Be U'Nique

### Antoinette B. Seawood

I have a story to tell you about a woman who was traumatized and mistreated by her family. As a girl, she was lonely, a motherless and fatherless child, and she always felt as though she was being suffocated, with no air to breathe.

Her father was murdered by the Chicago Police Department when she was two years old, and though her mother was technically alive, the streets had her tied up and held hostage, a lost soul who didn't know night from day. Every day the girl silently cried out for help, wishing someone would save her from her horrible nightmare, an endless one of missing what she needed to stay alive. Her only safe and happy moments were when she dressed in her grandmother's clothing and shoes. Those jazzy bits of fabric and leather gave her a tiny bit of the security she missed.

Despite her attempts to be accepted by her peers, she never was. No matter how she tried, they just used her to do the dirty work they weren't brave enough to do. She both envied and hated the children who did have parents, and she wanted to make those kids feel the pain she felt as a virtual orphan. That's ugly, but it's true. She was aware enough to fight within herself to keep from following her parents' path. She didn't want to fall into the streets, the hands of evil, or her enemies.

> Live every moment as if it were your last.

Yes. The story is true. And what's also true is that girl was me.

I tried to grow up fast and leave my childhood behind. When I was only 15, I had a child just to have someone of my own to love, and I made sure I loved Taquaja in the way I wished my parents had loved me. I made sure my daughter's father was a part of her life, too, right up until he was killed when she was only 10 years old. Suddenly, I was left to deal with a child who didn't understand why someone would take her father. Unfortunately, I didn't have any answers for her.

She followed the path I traveled at her age, becoming angry, resentful, and distant to others because she had no father. Our lives spiraled out of control and we became homeless. Taquaja and I lived mainly in our car, with my daughter sleeping in my back seat some nights and me awake watching her sleep to ensure she wasn't harmed. Other nights, we found someone's house where we crashed, and where I could finally sleep the entire night.

No matter where we spent our nights, every morning I showered and got dressed for work as if my life was on track and I had it all together. No one knew I had laundry bags in my trunk, full of clothes for Taquaja and me. No one knew we had no permanent roof over our heads.

Though our situation improved, I kept my depression hidden and locked up for what seemed to be decades while I walked through life filled with my own anger, hurt, self-consciousness, and insecurity, all of the building blocks of my basic emotions, which caused me to lash out without ever knowing why.

I knew life was precious, but I had no gratitude for others or even for my own life. When I bumped into those uncomfortable thoughts, they caused me to pause, rollover, and move slowly away from reality like a turtle hiding in its shell.

I've been up and I've been down, and I feel no shame in admitting it.

Fast forward to 2016: I started a better job, Plant Coordinator, which I loved, but I was harassed by all-male management and co-workers soon after being employed with the company. Mind you, I was the sole woman in my department at the time because the only other one quit a couple of months after I started.

In 2018, I became sick and was rushed to the emergency room, and then admitted into the hospital.

When I returned home, I was sick for days and barely could move because of all the medications they gave me.

For months, the medications made me worse, not better. I started to hallucinate and became irritable for absolutely no reason. I vomited all my food right up, and I lost 55 pounds in less than three months. As badly as I wanted to heal, I couldn't because my mental capacity seemed to be failing me; I suddenly had memory loss, vision problems, and couldn't read.

The doctors took me back down memory lane for a diagnosis. According to them, the disease may have been affecting me for quite some time. I underwent biopsies and tons of blood tests before I was diagnosed with simple—but deep—depression. Medication included steroid drops, plus pills and gospel music to relax me. I couldn't drive so I was homebound for a while. My daughter assisted me with reading and anything I had to physically look at to comprehend or respond.

Imagine watching TV when all of a sudden your body gets hot as a fire pit and you hear voices screaming *KILL YOURSELF!* Several times it happened to me, and I'd run out of the house in terror, yelling for my daughter. Taquaja would run to my rescue, asking what's wrong, holding me while I was crying, and trying to explain the feeling of black air filled with fiery torches and evil voices surrounding me.

It was a scary situation, but God protected me and found a way to ease the pain and fear as I healed. After a few months, I was able to return to work. Though the tension and harassment continued, I wasn't going to give in and quit as they wanted me to do. Unfortunately, my employer increased the pressure the next year.

In 2019, my freedom completely vanished, and my stress level increased because I was working 13-hour shifts, seven days a week. I was never scheduled for time off; if I switched with someone so I could be off, I was told I wasn't my own boss and that was forbidden.

When I fell ill again, I had to be admitted into a hospital for 30 days to treat my depression, complicated by alcohol abuse. I was sure I was dying. Everything felt wrong. I felt lost, I felt unwanted, I felt neglected, and I felt every feeling that was unhealthy and led me to want to give up on myself and my family. I caused my family turmoil and pain. I almost ended my life.

Thanks to God, I found serenity instead. I chose to take my life back and live for *my*self. I chose to do what made *me* happy, and I stopped allowing others to destroy me mentally.

My recovery included learning meditation, which was hard to do because my mind wouldn't stop wandering and talking gibberish.

My recovery included learning that my mother's absence wasn't because she didn't love me, but because she'd made a choice she thought was best for me. (She's part of my life now and tells me daily how much she loves me!)

My recovery included a sister who made it a point to check on me, tell me everything was going to be okay and told me she loved me after every conversation.

My recovery couldn't have happened without a daughter and a grandmother who never left my side and told me daily how much they loved me, no matter what storms battered our lives.

My recovery included closing myself up in my closet to get to know myself again, learning who I was outside of what I had been through. I dug up every horror story I had encountered and confronted it head-on and then forgave myself and those who hurt me. I learned to get back up and keep moving forward from past pain.

My recovery included psychotherapy, which helped a tremendous amount. Therapy helped me realize the majority of my hurt and pain came from my childhood and I'd never let it go. I stopped letting the past determine how I'd react in the days to come.

Part of learning to cope and deal with it all has been learning to eat properly, exercise, get an adequate amount of sleep, and do my best to be the best I can be.

I also learned a key lesson: *It's imperative to focus on what's important to you and your future.*

In 2020, my eyes swelled and turned bloodshot red every other day, and the doctors thought I might go blind. That scared the crap out of me because nobody knew what was wrong. Finally, they had a diagnosis: I had an unusual version of sarcoidosis, a rare autoimmune disease. It is not a curable disease; it's chronic and sometimes fatal. In my case, it's horribly painful and sometimes I can barely walk.

Because I was unable to work, I was soon about to lose everything. My Infiniti was going to be repossessed, and I was on the verge of being evicted from my house. I was terrified of being homeless again. Though I called around to every governmental and non-profit resource I could find, nobody could keep me from being evicted from my house and having to move, no matter how well I kept in contact with the owners.

My crisis woke me up on so many levels. I told myself I was *not* going to be homeless. I was *not* going to be without transportation. I *was* going to rise from these ashes. I was going after *everything* my heart desired!

At that point, I decided to put my best foot forward and pursue *my* dreams. It was time to finish recovering from my depression, time to overcome my anxiety. It was time to go after a dream of mine. I was in a place I thought I would never come back from, but *I made it!*

Some friends turned their backs on me, but I am grateful for the ones who didn't. I stepped outside my comfort zone, filled out an application for a *bigger* house in a *better* neighborhood, applied for a car loan for a car that I didn't think I would get—and this all with *no* job or income of my own. I prayed and talked to the Universe, and I was blessed with a wonderful four-bedroom, three-bathroom house (one bedroom less than I had before, but one more bath), plus a bigger backyard and a big deck. My family, my five dogs, and I *all* are happy and comfortable.

I am now an entrepreneur, and my mission is to speak to society through my brand. I joined Tori Belle as an affiliate for magnetic lashes and started my own lash business, *Be U'Nique Too Lashes*. I designed and launched my shoe collection, *Serenity*, which includes a heel collection that will be launching very soon. I put my shoe collection under my very first LLC, Naturally U'Nique, which I realized needed to be created.

I rebranded my home-based travel agency and put it into an LLC also, building my iBüümerang business to create more generational wealth for my 25-year-old daughter, who's my rock and always keeps me on my toes. She's the reason I press so hard to make my businesses successful, because I know she is always watching me.

This isn't all! I'm also in the process of starting my own clothing line. My "mocks," or mock-up illustrations, are designed and ready to go. The clothing will also be in my Naturally U'Nique line. While branded slightly differently, the clothes are designed with my brand and vision in mind.

I know when you look good, you feel good. I want to take travel and fashion to a place filled with adventure, thrill, peace, euphoria, creativity, and everything rejuvenated. We might miss a flight or leave a bag, but boarding that plane brings our minds at ease and relieves that tension. Buying a new pair of shoes or a new piece of clothing is where the heart lies as we strut the streets with a huge smile and a soul filled with confidence and pride.

Going through life's traumas taught me who I am as a woman and a person. I have learned to never take life for granted and to appreciate what I have, no matter how big or small. My goal is to continue to lend a helping hand to those who allow me to assist them in releasing their pain, anger, and hurt.

My speaking up about what I've been through has already sparked the fuel in others' lives, and it will continue to do so. My experiences can allow you to see that life isn't over and remind you to keep pushing forward.

My experiences can remind you to treat yourself kindly and to respect yourself in the most valuable way. Don't dump your bad thoughts, your poison, your disrespect on yourself. Learn from my example to eat like a human being mentally, physically, and emotionally and *not* as an animal. Learn from my example to surround yourself with people who see value in you, as much as you do in them.

Take my example and give yourself a chance at whatever it is you want to do, instead of saying *I CAN'T*. Use my example and learn to set goals that you can stick to as you align them with your life and not someone else's.

I can't help you with stress because I haven't mastered coping with it just yet, but I am working hard toward preventing that demon from entering my life. My goal is to help others eliminate stress and anxiety while becoming successful in whatever it is they see fit. Now I have my first calling in my life, and I plan to fulfill every future calling that comes my way.

My vision is for you to overwhelm depression and anxiety with the positive aspects of life. Focus on the authenticity of what life has really given you. Society tends to keep us sheltered and silent from speaking out on not being perfect and having mental issues and illnesses, but now is the time to know you are not alone and it's okay to talk about it! Let it out! Be the change that saved someone else's life. Focus on where you were and how you overcame challenges as an individual. You in turn will be able to help others overcome their challenges.

Life isn't easy, but it's what we make of it. So make the best of what you have and live your life to the fullest. Live every moment as if it were your last. When you walk, hold your head high, your chin higher, and strut as though the world is yours, with no worries! Don't let anyone, man or woman, poison your soul with negativity, self-doubt, self-pity, or shame.

Let those fears go. *Imagine* you're climbing into your 18-wheeler, running every stop sign, and driving a hundred miles per hour over the speed limit! Don't stop until you reach your goals! Grab hold of life and convert it into something magical. Reach for the stars, and choose the best ones.

And, while you're enjoying this wonderful, fulfilling life, Be U'Nique.

*Be you!*

# Author's Notes

I am a 41-year-old African-American female CEO and owner of Naturally U'Nique LLC, U'Nique Getaways LLC, and Be U'Nique Too Lashes. In my previous corporate life, my background was manufacturing and logistics, and my professional roles include secretary, administrative assistant, supervisor, team leader, account manager, and coordinator.

My strengths and reputation are in training, teamwork, leadership, and advanced system and software skills.

Because I've always had a passion for helping others, I make a point of lending a hand to help resolve situations I encounter. Once a crisis is averted, I take the next step and help create a game plan so everyone can make the best of any situation.

My goal as a leader is to make sure everyone I work with is safe, has what they need to complete their responsibilities and tasks, and understands and follows the protocols. Being passionate about what I do makes it easier to sustain my long-term performance goals.

I enjoy volunteering for the cancer society, and homeless and battered women shelters. Recently, I've added mentoring and counseling roles to help those with depression and anxiety. Doing so allows me to help in areas I feel strongly about, and replenish the strength, courage, dignity, and self-confidence that were taken from me as a woman and human being. The knowledge that I can help another person overcome some of the same issues and fears I once had overwhelms me with joy.

I was born in Oak Park, Illinois, and attended Proviso East High School, The Academy Of Scholastic Achievements, and Triton College. My daughter, Taquaja Tolliver, my grandmother, and I live in Chicago, Illinois, with our five dogs. I make time for skating, bowling, traveling, jumping rope, designing, mentoring, and challenging myself to overcome my fears. My time is *now*.

## Contact Information

| | |
|---|---|
| **Email:** | antoinette@naturallyunique.net |
| | (for business purposes) |
| | info@naturallyunique.net |
| | (for product information) |
| **Facebook:** | Antoinette Seawood |
| | Naturally U'Nique |
| | U'Nique Getaways |
| **Websites:** | www.naturallyunique.net |
| | www.uniquegetaways.net |
| | www.beuniquetoolashes.com |
| **Twitter:** | ANTOINETTE SEAWOOD@ |
| | buniquegetaway |
| **Instagram:** | be_unique_too |
| **TikTok:** | beuniquetoo |
| **LinkedIn:** | linkedin.com/in/uniquegetaways` |

Chapter 14

# Your Life Is Not Beyond Repair

### Andre Nero

Throughout my life, I've been the black sheep of my family, but that was never my intention. When I was still in my teens, I survived a series of unfortunate and excruciatingly public events that forged my essence and my mindset.

In 2017, I published *Changed at the Altar,* a memoir covering those events in depth. Many of my readers have asked me, *Why are you so transparent about your life?* I didn't write those words—or these!—to make you feel sorry for me, but with the hope, you'll draw strength from not only me but the life-altering stories that made me into the person I am, with the mindset I harness for manifesting good.

With this chapter in *The Power of Mental Wealth,* I hope to continue the process and demonstrate to you there's nothing new under the sun. Bad things happen, and you don't need to react with embarrassment or anger. Whatever happens to you can be tempered and improved by your outlook on life.

When I was 13, my outlook was sunny and naïve. I fell in love with Samantha from the moment I saw her in the middle school cafeteria. Once our friends finally forced us to speak to each other after weeks of being shy and making googly eyes at each other, we became inseparable, and from the time we were 13 until we were 19, we saw each other practically every day. We were sure we were a match made in heaven.

*Your positive thoughts can catapult you into a different stratosphere.*

I'd walk Samantha home every day after school to make sure she made it there safely. When we weren't together, we talked to each other for hours on the phone until we fell asleep. There was no such thing as mobile phones then; we used payphones and phones that were attached to the wall with long curly cords.

It took a while before I met her parents because we were afraid of what they might say because we were so young. Her mother and stepfather were the assistant pastor and first lady of a small suburban-area church, so impressing them was important but no easy task. As our love grew and it was clear their daughter was in a serious relationship, they wanted to know who I was. Her parents dismissed our relationship as puppy love, and they were sure it wouldn't last more than a month or two.

Putting the cart before the horse, I asked Samantha's mom and stepfather for her hand in marriage when we were fourteen, and they laughed at me. Once the laughter was over and they acknowledged my seriousness, they agreed if we were still together when we were sixteen, they'd give us permission to become engaged.

We had no doubts about our future together, and when we were just sixteen, we became engaged on Christmas night. We had a party at her parent's house, with our families in attendance.

We tried to be adults when it came to finances, talking about our future and planning for security for us and the many children we hoped to have. To help Samantha feel secure and trusted, I gave her money from every paycheck I earned, and she deposited it into a savings account at her bank for our life together after marriage.

I was well-known in our neighborhood because I'd founded and was running a large choir, Voices of Inspiration, with 179 active participants. Life wasn't all music, love, and happiness, though. I had a significant problem at school because I was failing all my academic subjects horribly. It was a real issue for me because I was doing the work but was getting D's and F's. On the surface, it looked as though I was uncaring and calm about my failing scores, but that wasn't the case. I was being eaten alive on the inside because I couldn't understand why hours of study, and even extra tutoring, didn't help.

I didn't have a clue about where to turn for help; my mom was working three jobs to keep food on the table, I was working at a newspaper company to help with bills, and whenever I did get a glimpse of my mom when she was home between shifts, she'd be sleeping for an hour or two before it was time to go to the next job.

Every time my teachers notified my mom of my failing grades, she'd punish me. Everyone assumed I wasn't applying myself, yet the teachers kept passing me because I had a great attitude, and I was known and appreciated for Voices of Inspiration. They empathized with me in many ways, but they didn't help me figure out a solution to my problem.

The embarrassment factor caused me to keep my situation a closely guarded secret. The only person to know the full extent of my failure was Samantha, and she didn't know how to help. When a new counselor of Hispanic descent was hired, she looked at my scores and got to work. After a little research, she quickly pulled my mom into a one-on-one meeting to suggest that I be tested for a learning disability.

My mom instantly rejected the idea and swore I was just lazy, but the counselor begged her to let me take the test. We were all shocked when I tested so high for learning disability—my score was off the charts. (That's not a good thing, unfortunately.)

I was diagnosed with "ADHD, Combined Type." Because there were no options to help me at my school, I transferred to an out-of-town military school, which seemed at the time to be my only way forward.

Leaving school brought up many uncomfortable questions from my peers, both about leaving and why I was discontinuing the choir. To save face, I just lied and told them I was enlisting in the military.

What appeared to be a life blow turned out to be a blessing in disguise. Not only did I figure out my learning curve, but the military school gave me the opportunity to tap into a different kind of leadership ability. It was a bonus that I was able to graduate with a GED six months before all of my peers graduated from high school.

Samantha waited for me while I was away, and my family was proud of the turnaround I had made.

Eventually, I told my friends my real reason for leaving, one of the many weights I wanted to lift off my shoulders. They laughed and understood why I had to go that route, and to my surprise, some of them already knew why I left.

Once I graduated, I had a sense of accomplishment, and the mind-wrecking self-defeated gloom-and-doom thoughts of failing were behind me. My future was now in sight, but it didn't include higher education. In my mind, I'd barely made it through high school, and I wasn't interested in facing more stress and havoc. Emotionally, college was not an option.

With my head clear, I could focus on a future with Samantha. Things were looking brighter, and our plans were getting more complex. We wanted a big family—I mean stair-steppers—ten children in all.

Because I had deep ties to our church, people speculated that I would become a pastor and later a bishop. Our wedding date was looming, but there were still eight degrees of separation because I didn't feel physically close enough to her. My mom, two brothers, and I had always attended church in Chicago, but now

I was of age to go to whatever church I wanted. I opted to leave my home church to go to her church, where her parents worked, and which was also closer to home.

Her small church welcomed me with open arms as a new member. Little did I know that tension behind the surface was building up and life was about to take a dramatic turn for the worse.

Valentine's Day was approaching. I have a creative mind, though a little off the wall sometimes, and I thought it'd be a great idea to create a huge, customized, humorous, and loving Valentine's card for Samantha. With the pastor's approval, I mounted it onto the front door of the church.

Everyone appreciated and laughed at the card, including Samantha's stepfather—everyone except her mom. Why, might you ask? I had included her entire name, her real last name, the full name I'd always known her by. I had zero knowledge that she'd been using her stepfather's last name at church.

To her mom, using Samantha's full legal name was disrespectful, embarrassing, and had undone everything she'd built as a respected leader and wife within this church. My mother-in-law-to-be yelled, pushed me into the church office, threatened me, and finally promised that I would *not* be marrying her daughter.

It was all downhill from there.

At that point, the wedding was scheduled to take place in only a few months Things swiftly grew more uncomfortable with every stressful encounter with my fiancée's mother. Both Samantha and I were anxious to get married and get beyond the anger and recrimination. So I thought.

Her mom was laser-focused on making sure she made me feel bad every moment and reminded me she would stick by her words as it came down to the final days before the wedding. Her stepfather stayed out of her way to avoid conflict. He'd had years of practice doing that, I suspect.

Finally, we reached the day we would no longer be two, but one. Our wedding was to begin at seven o'clock in the evening. The church was wedding-ready, and gifts had been sent by friends and family from all over the country.

The head pastor was excited and ready to marry us; my mother was there, and my fiancée's stepfather was also in attendance. However, Samantha's mother was not there, and so, most importantly, neither was my bride. My almost-father-in-law asked me if I had heard anything because he was also confused. The wedding guests began to worry as the night wore on, and I had to muster up the strength to calm everyone down and convince them to stay, and at the same time, I tried to appear unbothered.

By ten o'clock, Samantha and her mother still had not arrived. Her stepfather offered his apologies and gathered his belongings to leave.

I started the service, singing songs and holding everyone hostage until midnight. At that point, I had no choice but to let everyone leave. People attempted to console me as they walked out, and I did my best to hide my pain and seem confident and calm.

After everyone left, I remained in the church for a long while, full of misery and depression. Samantha's mother's words were ringing in my head over and over. I had not married her daughter, just as she'd threatened.

Worse yet, as I learned, Samantha actually married another man on our wedding day, and *he* was a pastor. The news destroyed me emotionally and mentally and broke my heart. It had reduced me down to my lowest denominator, with seemingly no way to recover.

Hold on—our drama wasn't over yet. A week after her secret wedding, Samantha left her husband and came back to me. I still loved her, and despite my hurt, I welcomed her back into my heart.

But my decision to take her back became a costly one, and not just financially.

Our first stop was her bank, where all the money I'd given her over the years was safe in an account, ready to fund our new lives together. We slept in the car, waiting for the bank to open so we could withdraw the funds. Both exhausted and emotionally wrung out, we overslept. Two hours after the bank's opening, we went in to withdraw the money, only to find out we were at least an hour too late.

At this moment, I discovered Samantha didn't have her own account; it was a joint account with her mother, who had come in and withdrawn every penny. An infinite cloud of darkness hovered over my head for the next few years; a different me started to grow.

Samantha and I began our lives together in a way I'd never imagined, cohabitating, not married to each other, with her married to another man. We were living under a cloud of shame. I left the church, and emotionally, I became dead to the world. All I did was work multiple jobs to try and build back our nest egg. My family, including my mom, no longer wanted anything to do with us as the drama intensified.

The last straw was when the pastor Samantha had married behaved in a very un-Christian way and threatened my mom. I'd had enough, I was completely unhinged from being overworked and exhausted, and at that moment I lost whatever marbles remained. My non-violent retaliation landed me an eight-year prison sentence, and the community I served was in complete shock at my misdeeds. Samantha left me again.

In prison, I was no longer in control of my own life. I began to deteriorate. I didn't talk for six solid months because I was pretty confident my life was over and I didn't care. I had no hope for the future and over a short period, my physical appearance and demeanor became hardened and unrecognizable to anyone, even my family.

Then one day, a guard didn't act like any of the other guards. He spoke to me as a human and not as a criminal in the system. Though I kept my hard expression, he saw something in me and continued to speak life into me. He looked past my faults and saw the God in me.

The guard told me nobody ever just wakes up in greatness, and even a just man falls seven times. He encouraged me to pick myself up and stop feeling sorry for myself. He said I was still physically imprisoned because my mind was imprisoned. That statement broke something in me, and my *aha!* moment arrived.

Listening to this kind and human guard was the first time in a long while that I felt whole again. I began to write and speak affirmations every morning and worked on myself unceasingly.

Suddenly and surprisingly, I was released much sooner than anticipated. I believed I manifested or willed that release into existence.

When I came home, the life I'd known no longer existed. My new life was anything but perfect—subpar employment, unfair housing treatment, two bankruptcies, homelessness, and credit woes. I still dare to believe my attitude about life played a significant role in what happened next.

I paid my debt to society, as they say, and that had been going on two decades at the point of my breakthrough. Even though some events came close to breaking me, they didn't destroy me, and with the proper positive mindset, I lacked nothing and made it through any obstacle that came my way.

I am beyond pleased to share that though it took a long time, I've now cleared my records.

I've attended three colleges and have earned degrees in criminal justice and business administration, and an executive master's degree in public service and administration—with excellent grades.

I have received recognition from Radio One and the NAACP Image Awards, am mentoring youth, and running a successful business.

I've written one book and am now completing two more, one a co-authorship with the incomparable Les Brown and Johnny Wimbrey. I have had more than 350 opportunities to share my stories on platforms around the country.

I don't share any of these details to boast, but to emphasize that your positive thoughts can catapult you into a different stratosphere. It may not happen overnight, but keep believing that it can happen, and it will!

You may have many dark days, you may feel like giving up and throwing in the towel, but keep your chest out and your head held high. What you think and say about yourself will manifest eventually, and no matter where you are in your life, it is never beyond repair.

You don't have to see it to believe it, but you must believe it until you see it! I'm using my story to hopefully and prayerfully get you and your mindset onto the next level. Respect the process; there are always problems, and there is *no* process without pain. Problems produce pain, pain produces praise, praise produces purpose, and purpose produces promise. I'm here to tell you that you can never get to the promise without the pain.

You really are not defined by your past, employment, social status, or social media followers, but by your *self-worth*, the value you place in yourself. Also, continue to believe in your heart that you are worth more than you think because as you change your thinking, you change your life.

Discontinue using events from your past as stumbling blocks and start using them as stepping-stones, because who you were yesterday is not who you are today. You may have done what they say you have, you may have been where they say you've been, but you are not *who* they say you are. You are who *God* says you are!

# Author's Notes

Born and raised in Chicago, I now live in Dallas.

## Contact Information

Email: texastakeovercajf@gmail.com
Facebook: AmericasGotNero
Instagram: AmericasGotNero
Twitter: AmericasGotNero

Chapter 15

# Take Pain By The Hand And Walk Into Greatness

### Elyse Arroyo Peña

"The mind can be a bad neighborhood," my aunt often said as she tapped her temple. I know this is true, now more than ever. In my three decades, I have learned a lot about life, loss, happiness, and success. Most importantly, I learned how strongly our mental state affects us when life gets tough.

I hope you will gain some enlightenment from the tools that helped me through the darkest times of my life. I know through my work in business and service that the tools I've shared have helped others gain more confidence, courage, and left some believing *If she can, then so can I!*

By leveraging my tools, I have felt more happiness and fulfillment, more success in my career, and I've achieved a mental awareness more valuable to my success than anything else. And this is all thanks to a friend I call "grief."

We'll talk a little more about my new friend a little later, but first I'll introduce myself. If you ask me who I am, I'll answer *many things*. I'm a mother. A wife. A boss. A servant leader. I'm also a daughter, sister, and friend. I'd like to believe I have a pretty normal life. Like the rest of you, I hurt, I'm emotional, and most of all, I am strong, even when I don't believe myself to be.

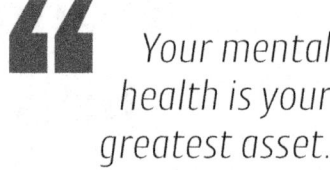

*Your mental health is your greatest asset.*

I've learned our personal trials and tribulations drastically impact our mental health and mindset, no matter what spiritual, religious, or emotional support we have. If we fail to "feel" ourselves as we work through these issues, we miss out on life's most important lessons and experiences. Life does not just happen *to* us; it happens *for* us.

I believe if we want true happiness, success, and fulfillment, we first must recognize we're students of our own lives. We need to understand our past and recognize we are the sum of all of our experiences.

I was born and raised in the South Bronx. All of my grandparents are from Puerto Rico, and they moved to the mainland for better opportunities. Ensuring their sacrifices were not made in vain has always been a guiding force in my life. My parents did everything they could to give my sister and me a solid foundation.

My mother is a nurse, but because they wanted the best for my sister and me, she stayed home while we were growing up in the toughest neighborhood in New York City.

Because of the home my parents created and the youth group I joined when I was young, I did not fall victim to the many vices available in my neighborhood. The youth group is still run by the Franciscan Friars of the Renewal, a fraternal community within the Catholic Church. These pious and authentic men in grey robes were my first-ever mentors. Not only did they teach me my Catholic faith, they also provided a clean and safe environment where I could be myself and speak my mind.

The environment my parents and the friars created and fostered allowed me to truly be a child and afforded me the ability to dream.

**Environment.** As an adult, I look back on the foundation my life was built upon and I'm able to recognize what will be my first piece of advice to you: *Environment is everything.* The people you surround yourself with matter! The places you go matter! All things around you influence your inner voice, and that is the first thing impacting your mental health and mindset.

When you surround yourself with positive, genuine, loving, and successful people, you become a sponge for all their positive energy. When you go to places that help feed joy and purpose, the settings help facilitate inspiration, desire, and life. These places can be anywhere; you might find them to be the gym, the library, nature, school, or even an imaginary destination reached through a good book.

If you're lucky, your special places may include that place your mind goes to when you are inspired—a true out-of-body experience. If you're able to achieve that kind of awareness, then you're starting off on the right foot when it comes to having true mental wealth.

**Mentors.** My next piece of advice comes in three parts. First, *get a mentor*. Second, get *many* mentors, in fact, and always be open to new ones. Third, never try to force the process of gaining a mentor. You want the relationship to be genuine and real.

A true mentor will help you open your mind and your perspective. A good mentor will show tough love when it's necessary, but also will never judge you. Mentors provide insight; you don't always agree with them, but that's the point. You only know what you know, and unless someone else opens your mind and teaches you more, your mindset and mental wealth will remain trapped.

My mentors have shown up during the times in my life when I needed them the most, and many are still showing up for me.

**Service.** My third piece of advice is *service*. Be in the business of service to others, whether it's in business, friendship, or companionship. When you begin to lose the notion of "what's in it for me," you'll see that your energy and efforts will be returned to you in many forms.

Through my youth group, I attended retreats where I had my first encounter with serving, not only serving in my faith, but also serving others through my voice.

The retreat director, Angela Scannapieco, eventually became my spiritual mentor. Many times she asked me to give my personal testimony to a room of teens and young adults, and sometimes the room was packed with hundreds of people. I remember feeling nervous yet ultimately exhilarated over the opportunity to share and serve others through my words.

After participating in a few retreats, I was asked to join the team that organizes and conducts them. We organized retreats throughout the state of New York, meeting people from every possible circumstance. I finally learned the definition of fulfillment: *Fulfillment can only truly come from an act of selflessness and a true act of service to others.*

That's when I found my calling and realized what I wanted to do for the rest of my life—to serve and lead others to love, joy, and fulfillment.

In the corporate world, I learned when I serve my team by helping them meet their goals, their accomplishments are mine as well. When I serve my family by helping my children learn new accomplishments, I celebrate in their joy when they are proud of themselves. When I serve others by sharing my story, I share in their hopes and perseverance.

**My journey through grief.** My new friend—grief—first began to show itself on 9/11 when I realized my father, a union electrician, was sched-uled to work near the World Trade Center in lower Manhattan that day. The school staff brought the students to the school cafeteria and I grieved as I watched my friends get picked up one by one. Then I felt such joy when my father walked into the cafeteria to find me; it turned out he'd called in sick that morning and was safe at home.

High school came faster than expected, and it was frightening. I wanted to do well in my studies and find a place to fit in at DeWitt Clinton High School, a well-known public school in the Bronx that had been a former boys' school for 100 years. High school became a little less scary when I discovered the school's Junior Reserve Officers Training Course (ROTC), where I found more mentors and friends; many are still a part of my life.

ROTC introduced me to leadership and effective communications and gave me confidence. The guidance of teachers and coaches took my head out of the clouds and introduced me to reality, discipline, and accountability. I learned I can overcome anything and do anything, regardless of what's going on in my life.

That mindset was very important to me during the great recession because we lost our family home and had to move across town, away from our church and my friends. It was the first real loss I had ever experienced. I continued to attend the church youth group in my old neighborhood, and I remember how wonderful the friars and everyone in the group were to my family during that difficult period. I know that's what kept my family's loss from breaking me—all the strength and support I received from the youth group on top of the firm foundation I had been given by my family.

When I graduated from high school in 2007, I was excited to begin college. I had been accepted by Utica College, which is affiliated with prestigious Syracuse University. But the recession was looming, and by the time

I was supposed to leave for my first semester, I realized my family couldn't afford the school. I was devastated but picked myself up and enrolled in Lehman College, a senior college of the City University of New York, which is where I met my future husband, Erodes Peña. That meeting helped teach me that nothing is an accident.

The recession continued to affect our family, and a couple of years after losing our house, we were behind on our rent and lost our apartment. My sister and I decided to stick together, and we were homeless until our grandmother took us in.

I remember trying to go to class, being in a fog, feeling numb. Stress and depression crept in, and I had to take a year off from school. I could feel no emotion on the inside. Sometimes I wished for sadness because that would mean I could at least feel an emotion. That young dreamer and ambitious servant leader was nowhere in sight during that time.

I worked full-time while I was in college, and I graduated in 2014, three years later than planned. I piled a lot of shame on myself for not graduating on time, and I couldn't stop comparing myself to my peers, whom I felt were so far ahead of me. I was self-conscious and overly critical of myself. I truly was not happy even though I had overcome so much. All I knew was I had to keep pressing forward and live on.

When Erodes and I married in August 2016, it was one of the happiest days of my life. He had supported and loved me during my weakest, most depressed, and most self-loathing times, and I knew our marriage would be an important foundation in our lives. That foundation turned out to be crucial, because over the next four years I was tested by grief and tragedy that would break almost anyone.

Just three months after our wedding, I woke up to several missed calls from Erodes. When I picked up, I immediately knew something was wrong because he is so patient and soft-spoken whenever something serious is occurring. He gently told me my father had passed away.

You see, grief, *true* grief, is not something that comes and goes. It is part of everything for the rest of your life. It's in all of your memories and in the missed present and future of that person. What made my experience with grief even more complicated was that I had my first child, Brie, a year later. I couldn't grieve the way I should have because I had a newborn. Though I didn't know it then, I was also suffering from postpartum depression.

The following year I lost my Uncle Pablo, who'd been a huge pillar of support in my life. On the inside, I regressed to a place I don't wish upon anyone. I couldn't show my pain and difficulty coping on the outside because I was known for being such a strong person; I was also expecting my second child, Noah.

During my dark time of loss and poor mental state, it shouldn't be surprising that my career also took a negative turn. I didn't hold myself accountable and wasn't receptive to feedback when my actions impacted my team, and it burned out many work relationships.

Unfortunately, my poor mindset didn't improve until I found mentors in Kealy and Jeff, two of my bosses. They genuinely believed in me and saw my potential, and they helped me recognize opportunities and focus on my strengths. The investment they made in me turned my career around and also helped me progress in my own personal development.

As a result, my salary increased, I was promoted, and I'm on a path for future promotions. This would not have been possible without their support as I worked to overcome my negative mindset.

When I lost my spiritual mentor and second mother, Angela, in 2019, her death was an important touchpoint for me. My grief after her death was very different, much healthier, because I finally realized I needed to feel all my pent-up pain and sadness. Thanks to this, I was truly able to begin the process of self-healing. I became more self-aware, and I started to identify all the things that no longer served me.

That was when I resolved to be kinder to myself. I changed the way I spoke to myself, and I also decided I was no longer going to diminish myself to appease any outside force, whether that be in my friendships, my family, or my career.

You see, sometimes tragic or painful events must happen to you before you can fully experience the shift that will calibrate your mindset in the right direction. In my case, it took multiple deaths of people whom I loved to mold me into the person that I am now.

Once I made this new shift in my mindset, I immediately started to experience growth in my personal life and my career. I was much less defensive and more receptive to the feedback and opinions of those who really mattered.

The results boosted my confidence. As my confidence grew, the voice in my head became kinder and kinder. The kinder voice gave me comfort and provided encouragement. Whenever fear and doubt entered my mind, I was able to handle it more rationally than I had before.

The birth of my third child, Luca, in December 2020, helped me see how far I had come in 21 months. Many things had come full circle for me at that point. I was able to center myself and trust my instincts. 2020 was a crazy year, full of unexpected turns thanks to the pandemic, and if I had been the same person I'd been during the first years of my grief, I would have been a dramatic mess, unable to make rational decisions. Anxiety would have eaten me alive as it had done on many past occasions. Instead, I was calm, calculated, and mindful.

When Luca was born, I felt a joy that was quite different than I'd felt after my first two. I had experienced so much loss over the years of their births that my postpartum depression blended with my grieving process. I hadn't been in a healthy place where any form of growth could occur.

As I looked back, I realized what's the most essential part of growing: *We have to make decisions.* We must decide to take our grief and pain with us into all that we are. We need to use our obstacles as lessons and live the life we know we deserve.

My grief taught me that life is for the living. It's too easy to be overly critical of yourself when you have a negative mindset, especially in the digital age of social media we have now. It's easy to focus on the bad when things aren't going right in your life. It's too easy to obsess on what others think of you, when in truth what really matters is what *you* think of yourself. Your mental health is your greatest asset, so take care of it.

No one else can possibly understand what it feels like to be *you*. This is why everything you say to yourself, what you pour into your mind, the way you associate with yourself *matters*. It matters whether you like and appreciate yourself or not.

I leave you with this: Allow yourself to be *you,* in all your greatness and all your imperfections.

# Author's Notes

I'm a motivational speaker, lifestyle blogger, and entrepreneur, and at the same time, I have a career leading in store operations for Target in the New York City metro area. Multi-tasking is nothing new for me because I began my career in retail management while still a full-time student, paying my own way through school as I earned a bachelor's degree in Political Science and Economics.

Another important part of my life for more than 20 years has been leading and mentoring young people. I've organized and have spoken at hundreds of youth events and retreats. My life's goal is to connect and reach people on a genuine level, serving them and leading them to love, joy, and fulfillment.

My husband, Erodes, and I live in the Bronx, New York City, with our three children.

## Contact Information:

**Email:** contactme@lifeinbellzz.com
**Website/Blog:** www.lifeinbellzz.com
**Instagram:** ellybellzz
**Facebook:** Elyse Arroyo Peña
**Twitter:** @ElyseArroyo

## Chapter 16

# Turn Your Pain Into Power

### Gavin Fortuin

Though all of the odds are stacked against them, the young men and women on the poverty-stricken Cape Flats of Cape Town, South Africa, manage to persevere. Working with them and expanding their horizons beyond hustling and crime fills me with humility and respect—and at the same time lifts my sense of self-worth and makes me feel alive.

Don't get me wrong. I don't claim to have it made. While I am headed to a place of significance, my journey still has a long way to go. What matters is I'm on that journey, and this is a big change from 20 years ago.

Then, my life was quite different, and I was in the same place as the young people I'm helping now. My Cape Town community took a very dim view of my teenage self and the company I kept. My friends and I were regularly confronted and questioned by the Neighborhood Watch, civilians who are trained to form a police-assistance league. Often, they had good reason to do so.

I was raised by a single mother, and my longing for a father made me vulnerable to predators. By the time I reached puberty, I'd been sexually molested more than once, including by a man who pretended to be a psychologist and performed various sexual acts on me. I tried to block the incidents out of my mind for years, but not very successfully. I felt self-hatred for letting someone control and use me.

> *Your destination is important, but the person you become along the way is much more valuable.*

By the time I reached high school, I was already creating wholesale havoc. My main objective was to make others sit up and take notice, and the main avenue for this was through mischief and crime. Even at school, gang activity and illegal substances were rife, and whenever anything went down, mine was one of the first names to be mentioned.

Somehow, I realized I shouldn't join an actual gang, but my good sense didn't extend to the company I chose. One of my close friends—we'll call him Denver—did become a gang member, and I was drawn into gang-related conflicts by default. I wasn't officially a gang member, but he and I were tight, and we enjoyed the havoc we wreaked together. Fights were a daily occurrence, and I loved the adrenaline and power that came with them. Denver ended up becoming a member of one of South

Africa's most notorious prison and street gangs.

One night in a park, a friend unexpectedly pulled out a revolver and started shooting. I ran for my life as the Neighborhood Watch returned fire, sending a rain of bullets from their semiautomatic pistols past my ears, creating a shower of sparks against a chain-link fence. I ran at full speed, though my adrenaline rush made everything seem to be happening in slow motion.

I should have been hit. Divine intervention protected me as I zigzagged through a jungle gym and sprinted to where I planned to scale the wall to safety. I never made it. Mid-jump, I was tackled from the side, and I spent the rest of the evening at the police station. Reckless as they might seem, episodes like this were par for the course during my teenage years.

I saw myself as beyond redemption, ready to "die a thug," even if not everyone saw me that way. At least one teacher didn't see me as a troublesome thug, but as a young man with potential. Whatever potential she saw in me totally eluded me. She comforted my mother when the principal finally declared me a "menace to society" and expelled me from school.

My mom needed the comforting because she knew she'd lost control of me and was sure things were about to go from bad to worse. Once I was home full-time, all of my time and energy was dedicated to obtaining and using drugs—plus the dishonest and underhanded activity that comes with drugs. I used it in my room, always with a cast of shady characters who saw my house as a safe place to use. Many nights my mom cried herself to sleep while a bunch of us were smoking meth and quaaludes mixed with weed in the next room. Once

I overdosed and only recovered by a miracle.

Shane, my cousin and level-headed best friend who often kept me out of trouble, died after I left high school. We'd been inseparable, and my world fell apart. I was unable to deal with grief and became even more self-destructive.

It seemed as if I was arrested for possession every other week, and often held for an entire weekend in filthy and louse-infested cells. It was clearly just a matter of time before I would be sent to prison.

Mom finally had enough and kicked me out of the house, unwilling to watch me turn into a hardened criminal. She had my younger sister to think of, and my toxic influence was undoubtedly influencing her. At least Mom didn't ban me from the property, so I wasn't completely homeless. I slept outside on a cold concrete slab at the back of the house, my clothes threadbare and my body reeking.

I'm glad Mom finally found the courage to put me out, because the concrete slab is where my life started to turn around. Lying there, I had an epiphany, and I asked myself, *Is this the life I was born for?*

My mom hadn't totally written me off, and when I said that I was ready to leave drugs behind, she helped get me into rehab for the first time. Yes, that wasn't my last treatment center. Relapse often comes with the territory. I benefitted from each stint and have no regrets. Rehab didn't just provide a space to detox and get clean, it was a place where I could start leaving my past behind.

A social worker I met during a rehab stint was the first person with whom I shared the guilt and shame from my past, stories of the people I had hurt, and of those who had damaged me. The healing I got from sharing it all with her was life-changing and made me realize forgiveness is necessary to become free and liberated as a person.

In my case, rehab was also where I began to look to the future, and where I first experienced the influence of positive role models. One of these was an entrepreneur and motivational speaker who, by mere coincidence, happened to be facilitating sessions at two of the rehabs I attended. I don't think he crossed my path twice just by chance.

I owe this man my life. I admired what I saw—confidence, insight, and a passion for helping young people—and I made it my business to stay connected with him. He became my first real mentor, and he coached me in becoming a public speaker and youth practitioner. His aggressive and high-intensity leadership style ensured that I developed a solid foundation so I would have the endurance for future challenges.

My mentor encouraged me to attend conferences, including the Millennium Development Goals and Pan African Leadership forum conferences, to speak at these events, and to ask good questions. He even gave me clothes from his own closet because I had nothing suitable. Walking this journey with him activated my passion, purpose, and assignment on earth.

I learned the value of a mentor and was fortunate enough to find others as I grew and developed as a person.

The impact and influence they have on my life shaped the man I am today. Under their guidance, I have learned to put God first in everything. Under their tutelage, I developed an appetite for reading leadership, personal development, and self-help books. They taught me to ask questions to expand my mind and foster a philosophical outlook on life. By watching them, I have seen the heart of activism and the desire to serve the community.

Most of all, they've been good friends to talk with, whether to lift my mood, enlighten me, or inspire me to search deep within myself. While I will not mention them by name here, they know who they are, and I am profoundly grateful for the time, influence, and value they continue to add to the person I am still becoming.

Here I'll share three foundational concepts which have changed and improved every aspect of my life. Fully grasping our *identity*, *purpose*, and *vision* are prerequisites to reaching our full potential.

## Identity: *Discover who you are*

Truly knowing ourselves becomes our foundation for self-mastery and success. We human beings are the only living creations that don't automatically mature to our fullest potential. A tree will grow until it can't grow any more, and an animal will develop until it can perform at its optimal level. However, we human beings criticize and judge ourselves for past mistakes, despite our infinite intelligence, and we stunt our own growth by punishing ourselves. We must become cognizant of the wealth we possess inside and realize that all we need to do is unfold like a flower in the morning, kissing the sun's rays. A bird's trust is not in the strength of the branch it's sitting on but in its own wings.

*You attract who you are* is one of the principles I live by. You attract everyone, everything, and situations to yourself like a magnet. The Law of Attraction created the person I am today. The evolution of the power of my thoughts has transformed my life and that of other families forever. When my personal philosophy transitioned from a victim mentality to an abundance mindset, I recognized my thoughts had created my world. I can become whatever I think about.

Our attitude—how we act, treat others, and interact in the world—is an indication of our belief system. Gradually, our character forms at a young age as we absorb every event, interaction, touch, and environment like a sponge. For instance, scientific studies show children growing up with parents who frequently argue and fight have mental health and cognitive problems, among other issues; their brain development is affected.

Awareness of your own insecurities, shortcomings, and limitations is important to recondition your mind to look at life from another viewpoint.

> *We don't see things as they are,*
> *we see them as we are.*
> **—Anais Nin**

Realize that you have the tendency to look and act according to your past experiences and pain. You must demystify bias, culture, traditions, and old habits to embrace the new uncharted frontiers of the future. You have the capacity to use mindfulness to acknowledge who you are now and then change yourself. You can transform like a butterfly going through its metamorphosis.

Being indecisive about who you are will lead to doubt; doubt will create fear. It's imperative to make a decision and draw the map for your journey to success, however you choose to define it. Think of making your decision as if you were starting a surgery. When a surgeon makes the initial incision, he definitively and cleanly makes his cut and doesn't look back.

Use that surgical approach when you make decisions—make it cleanly and don't look back with doubts and regrets. Otherwise, as you flounder and whack away at the decision-making process, reversing your path and changing your mind, you'll become known as untrustworthy. You'll also waste years of your life as you drift around from one direction and path to another, just like a piece of trash in the wind. Your decisions shape your destiny.

> *The only person you are destined to become is the person you decide to be.*
> **—Ralph Waldo Emerson**

As you make these conscious decisions about your future and begin moving down your new path, don't haul your dirty baggage from your past along on the trip. Hating and not forgiving others is like drinking poison and wishing someone else will die. Don't allow yourselves to hold onto hatred and resentment; they will consume all the joy inside you, and you'll also be nurturing health risks.

When you continue hating, the person you hate becomes your master and you will never experience true freedom. Cut the umbilical cord of hate and liberate and enlighten your spirit. Forgive, and you will operate from a point of strength and not weakness. In our vulnerabilities lies phenomenal power!

**Purpose:** *Identify your gift*

Your gift was given to you by the Divine, and it's something irrevocable that flows naturally through you without effort nor struggle. Your gift does not care how old or rich or poor you are, it will knock on the door of your heart until you decide to answer that call. The day you finally identify your gift and make use of it is the day you are truly born.

When you use your gift, your energy will flow with a higher vibration. That frequency will cause the universe to harmoniously flow to its source, back to you, but increased a hundred-fold. My search for meaning ended when I discovered my gift and purpose by using it and giving it away. My gift is not public speaking, nor is it the ability to facilitate youth programs. My gift is simply an ability to connect with people in a profound way, a way that makes everyone I encounter believe they matter and are special.

Too many people just merely exist, living life so cautiously that they might have not lived at all. They've never experienced true freedom, and for all purposes they're already dead. Don't waste your time with these people. Instead, identify those who are already using gifts similar to your own, and make it your life's mission to study them. Strategically maneuver yourself into their circles of influence and learn how they became successful. Success always leaves clues you can find and link together. Take what you learn and make it authentically your own.

Your next step is to find mentors who are already doing what you want to do and have become masters in their field and industry.

Don't make your goal simply to become "successful." Rather, become a person of *value*. Success will follow, because it will be attracted by the person you become.

Invest in yourself to make yourself more valuable. I practice what I preach, and I'm constantly investing in myself. Personal development is an intrinsic part of my journey to success. Reading books, exercising, eating healthfully, and guarding my heart and mind against toxic people are the habits I cultivate in my daily routine.

Excellence will be attracted by the person you become in your pursuit of unattainable perfection. Your destination is important, but the person you become along the way is much more valuable. Whenever passion fuels your purpose, you will have supernatural energy and a fire that burns within you, one that will never turn into ash.

Nothing worthwhile and great will ever be achieved if you stay within your comfort zone. Pain has a purpose. At some point, you'll suffer from one of two types of pain: the pain of discipline or the pain of regret. Regret is by far the most painful. When you try the unknown and suffer adversity, you'll be introduced to your true self. Use every bit of resistance, use every closed door to shape, prune, polish, and refine your gift to withstand future storms and turbulence.

Find the courage to turn your pain into power.

**Vision:** *Where are you going?*

When we study many great historical characters, we discover their vision allowed them to succeed despite overwhelming odds. When I returned from rehab, writing down my vision in a book was of utmost importance for my journey toward self-discovery and self-mastery.

My ultimate vision is to build a wilderness retreat on thousands of acres of land in Knysna, South Africa, or Alaska in the United States. I envision a self-sustainable, multi-level development/training institution creating employment for the youth of Africa and the world.

When you choose your vision, it will elect everything in your life—your friends, hobbies, income, health, lifestyle, and spouse.

When you imagine your vision, clarity is power, and the clearer you are, the more powerful you will be. Visualize specifically what you want in detail; picture the way it looks, tastes, smells, and feels, and identify the emotions attached to it. Then get to work with that end goal in mind.

Don't allow the limitations of your current situation to become the enemy of *your* vision. Imagination is my secret weapon, and it can be yours. With imagination, you have no ceiling and no limits, and only you can choose how far you want to go.

# Author's Notes

In addition to writing, my main focus is Change Agents Developing Youth Leadership (CADY Leadership, for short), an organization I founded in 2018. I'm also a motivational speaker and youth practitioner, and I serve as a consultant to a number of government and non-government organizations on social development and youth-related community issues.

My soon-to-be-published autobiography, *From the Gutters to the Podium: Your Pain Has a Purpose,* goes into more detail about the often-thrilling misadventures of my youth, how I overcame adversity, and the tools I mastered to turn my life around.

I live in Cape Town, South Africa, with my loving and supportive wife, Lynn. We are awaiting the birth of our child.

## Contact Information

| | |
|---|---|
| **Email**: | gavinsfortuin@gmail.com |
| **Websites**: | www.cadyleadership.com |
| **Facebook**: | Gavin Fortuin |
| | CADY Leadership |
| **Instagram**: | Gavin Fortuin |
| | CADY Leadership |
| **LinkedIn**: | Gavin Fortuin |

Chapter 17

# Believe in Your Own Success

### Leutisha D.W. Galloway

Success is near. Success surrounds us. Success is inside of us. It is who we are. *But*—success has to start within us. If *we* don't believe in our goals, who will? It has to begin with our mindset. It begins with what we believe. If we believe we can be successful, we *will* become successful. If we believe we're failures, then we will always be failures.

We must stop believing what *others* say we will become. In my case, I had to teach myself to stop listening to others and their negativity. When I was young, I told different people what I wanted to do when I grew up. Their responses were always negative.

They said I couldn't achieve my goals, that I'd never make it in life, and I was and would be nothing but a failure. They told me my goals couldn't be achieved, and they would believe my success only when they saw it. To hear those comments coming from their mouths tore me apart. How could people be so negative and hurtful?

At first, I believed them. They were watching me, sure I'd fail. And at that time, they were right. I *did* end up failing. I didn't believe I could do what I wanted to do.

Finally, I realized that if I was ever meant to succeed, I had to stop believing what the naysayers said. Instead, I should believe the voice inside me, the one I heard saying *Go for it!* After I stopped listening to negative people, I was relieved and surprised to learn their words no longer affected me. When I fell, I got right back up and tried again. Now, my watchers see me winning.

> *You can never become successful if you don't believe and follow what's in your heart.*

When I was in high school, I wanted to be a Spanish interpreter. When I told my teacher what I wanted to do, she was discouraging. She said I wouldn't make a lot of money being a Spanish interpreter because there weren't many Spanish speakers living in our area, and I should change my goals.

Instead of following my heart, I decided to listen to her, and I changed my major from Spanish. Much later, I discovered she was wrong and Spanish-language interpreters were and still are badly needed. Also, many businesses are looking for fluent bilingual people; speaking two languages is considered to be an asset in many careers.

It was too late for me, though. I had stopped studying Spanish intensively. Though I know Spanish and can say what I need to say conversationally, I haven't reached the level of fluency that I need for the language to be an asset to me in business, and definitely not as an official interpreter.

What would have happened if I had listened to myself and not my teacher, the person who didn't believe in me being able to use a second language as the basis of my career? I'll never know because that's not the path I took. My college major instead was social work. I came to that decision after taking a test to determine what kind of career would be good for me. Because I love helping people, social work seemed to be a natural career. But even though social work fit my personality traits, it really wasn't what I wanted to do.

After doing what everyone else wanted me to do too many times in my life, I finally made the decision to do what *I* wanted. There were times that I wasn't ready for the goals I wanted to achieve, but I had to learn to push myself to do what was needed.

A good example was in college after I finally convinced myself that yes, I'd become a social worker and began taking classes. A few classes in, I learned it was impossible to finish in four years because all required classes weren't offered every semester. I realized it'd take longer than planned, but I made the commitment and took as long as was needed to finish the degree, taking the classes when they were available. It's not what I wanted to do, but I knew I had to do it.

Later than originally planned, I graduated with my bachelor's degree in social work. Sometimes in order to get to the things we want, we have to do what we don't want to do.

After graduating, I was able to find a job in my field, working as a case manager at a domestic violence and homeless shelter for women. Though the work was rewarding and I enjoyed helping the women and children, I could sense something was missing.

During the next few years, I worked as a qualified mental health professional. I enjoyed helping people improve their lives and reach some normalcy, but even with the emotional rewards, I began to think it might not be the best career choice for me.

My third position was at an African-American museum, which was a fun job I really enjoyed. During the two years I kept the job, I started a technology business on the side, which quickly took off and became successful. Before long, my paid job at the museum was interfering with the work I needed to do with my side business. When I realized the extra work was about to kill me, I gave my notice.

You're probably asking yourself, "How is she successful if she always left her jobs?"

I had to find what was best for me. I realized that working a daily job, doing things I didn't choose to do, was not going to get me success. I learned that doing what I *enjoyed* doing was bringing me success. I had to start focusing on what made me happy, what made me into a better person, what pushed me to not give up.

In 2018, I wrote a book of poetry, *My Journey Through Life and Love*, about many of the different and painful challenges I had from middle school up until that point.

Back when I reached that difficult late-childhood, early-adolescent years, I started experiencing depression. I didn't understand at the time what I was going through, but I knew I was always unhappy. Because I was so shy and always worried about the way people would look at me, I had trouble making friends. Because I wanted to fit in, I started making myself out to be someone I wasn't. I was able to make a few friends, but too many people would pick on me, and it really hurt when they did the cruel things middle-school kids do.

I knew I had to learn how to cope with the pain, so I began writing. At first, my writing was just keeping a daily journal. Later, I began writing poetry. For the first few years, I wasn't writing enough to get a handle on my emotions and actions. I still fought back when I was picked on, and my school fights led to detentions, suspensions, and getting into trouble at home. Because I just wanted to fit in, I couldn't break the cycle. The longer it went on, the worse it became.

Much of the time I didn't want to go to school because I knew what was going to happen. I also didn't want to stay at home because I was always in trouble for my behavior at school. The constant punishments made me feel like my mother didn't love me. Much later, I realized she meted out those punishments not because she didn't love me but because she believed I was better than my actions. She wanted better for me.

With all the negativity and pain I was feeling at the time, I began to give up both on life and myself. I realized I didn't want to live anymore and decided to kill myself. My multiple suicide attempts were dramatic but unsuccessful: I attempted to stab myself in the chest several times, but I couldn't bring myself to actually do it. Something stopped me, and I just ended up crying and writing about it.

When I was a little older and began dating, I really struggled and kicked into full-bore depression. Dating and love never went the way I hoped. I imagined dating someone, things being great for us, and one day getting married and having children. Things were completely opposite of that. I had a few relationships where I was used and abused, and they made me feel even worse about myself.

For some silly romantic reason, I thought I really was in love during one bad relationship. My boyfriend lied to me, put me down, and just tore me apart emotionally without a thought or care. Many nights when I left his house I sped home way above the speed limit because I was so mad at him. One night I chose to take a dangerous and dark road from his house back to my house, and I started speeding, hoping I would hit something and kill myself. The car seemed to slow itself down before anything could happen. I realized I needed to leave him and never go back, but it took me a while to build up my strength to do that.

The relationship I had with my husband, Deon, didn't start off well. We dated on and off for about 10 years, starting when I was 20 and he was 17. Deon was very sweet, patient, quiet, and fun to spend time with, but he had no goals in life. The only thing he wanted to do was play video games all day. I just stayed sunk in my depression.

I'm sure you're asking yourself, "Why was she attracted to someone like that?" Deon and I grew up together, attending the same church. He had liked me since he was six years old and I was nine years old, and we always had a close friendship, a solid foundation for what followed. When we first started dating, he didn't even have his driver's license. He eventually got it after I nagged him about it for so long. I was focused on getting somewhere in life, and he had no ambition, which is what broke us up many times before we were finally married.

I became pregnant with our first child when we weren't officially dating, and that brought us back together because we both wanted to parent our child. I wanted to get married, but he didn't, and it slowly tore us apart again. I was also stressed by people not believing I was pregnant with his child. I was brokenhearted most of the time I was pregnant, and the thought of committing suicide crossed my mind once again. The only thing that kept me alive was the child I was carrying.

Things got better once the baby came and people could clearly see the baby was Deon's. We were still living apart, each with our own set of parents. I had our baby, Levi, with me every evening, and the baby would stay at Deon's house during the day while I was at work. I noticed there were things he didn't know about raising a child, and I argued with him about it.

Finally, we worked through all our differences. I pushed him to do better in life, and we even worked on his goals together. About two years later, we decided we really wanted to be together as a couple. When I became pregnant for a second time, we were ready to make it official and get married. Of course, some people didn't want us to get married, which caused more depression. By this time, we knew we were meant to be together and we weren't going to let anyone stop us. We finally stopped listening to the negative chatter, planned everything out, and got married.

If we had listened to the negativity and let them stop us, then we wouldn't be where we are now. It hasn't been easy, and we know we have to work at our marriage and relationship to have success in our marriage. The most important thing is we didn't give up on *ourselves*.

I couldn't let negativity or depression stop my success. Yes, it hurt, but I got through it. I had to smile through my pain when inside I was crying. No one knew what I was going through. Often you must go through pain to gain success. You will never become successful if you give up when things get hard. Also, you can *never* become successful if you don't believe and follow what's in your heart.

I grew up in Martinsville, Virginia, a city where a lot of families live in poverty and there's always some kind of violence happening. My goals in life are bigger than my city. I can't let the things that occur in my city stop me from becoming successful, but I can help make a difference in Martinsville. I'm working with a nonprofit that is trying to do just that and it's very rewarding.

Earlier in the chapter, I mentioned I now have a successful technology business that I focus on. It has given me the opportunity to learn what success is about. It's not about the money. It's not about doing fifty million things in life. It's about learning to be the best I can be. I do that by listening to daily inspirations, saying affirmations, and working on personal development. I have friends in the business who genuinely care about me. We call ourselves a "tamily," a team, and a family combined. Without their support, I couldn't be successful in this business. I love every one of them like they are my blood family.

If it weren't for God, I would have not made it this far. He stopped me from driving that knife through my chest many times. He stopped me from wrecking my car late at night after an evening of abuse from a boyfriend. He gave me a child to love when I needed it most. If it weren't for God, I would have killed myself, but He has something better for me to do.

I look back over everything that's happened in my life, and I can clearly see how my depression affected me. I couldn't make a positive change until I finally accepted the fact that listening to others' opinions caused my depression. Now my depression just lurks in the corner and doesn't affect me much. Now I focus on myself and what makes me happy; my state of mind is positive, and my success has blossomed.

My depression didn't stop me from having success. I still have my moments when I'm sad, but it's nothing like what I'd been through before. I have learned how to cope better with the challenges that face me. I have stopped letting how others feel about me get me down.

Depression is real, but you can get through it to the other side. You can become successful despite depression. Let me go a step farther: *Whatever* challenge you have had, you can still become successful. You don't have to give up because of the mistakes you have made in the past.

We all have made mistakes, and we can learn from each of them as we also learn not to repeat them. It's harder to become successful in life if we keep making the same mistakes over and over, don't you think? If you want success, get your mind right and get out of your comfort zone. Experience the power of mental wealth.

Go after it!

Most importantly, *be yourself*. You can accomplish your dreams because they're inside you. I've done that, and I am successful. You can be successful, too.

# Author's Notes

Leutisha Walker Galloway is a native of Martinsville, Virginia. She graduated from Radford University, where she received her bachelor's degree in Social Work. Leutisha is married and has two children. She is the author of the book called *My Journey Through Life and Love*. Leutisha is a Board Member for Uptown Partnership.

Leutisha Walker Galloway is a native of Martinsville, Virginia. She graduated from Radford University, where she received her bachelor's degree in Social Work. Leutisha is married and has two children. She is the author of the book called *My Journey Through Life and Love*. Leutisha is a Board Member for Uptown Partnership.

An accomplishment of which I'm very proud is my published book of poetry, *My Journey Through Life and Love*. I look forward to writing more books following the publication of *The Power of Mental Wealth*.

I'm very involved in my community and am a board member for Uptown Partnership, a nonprofit that provides advocacy and supports diversity in Martinsville, Virginia.

Recently, I founded and am CEO of Walker Galloway Industries, LLC, a technology and graphic design company providing products and services to businesses and individuals in our community.

I'm a native of Martinsville, where I still live with my childhood friend and husband, Deon, and our two children, Levi and Jabez.

## Contact Information

**Email:** leutisha88@gmail.com
**Website:** www.WalkerGalloway.com
**Instagram:** tishdani88
**Twitter:** Tish_Dances4GOD

Chapter 18

# Understand Your Power and Purpose

### Shirley Lancaster

According to the respected theologian, Dr. Art Lindsley, our image of God is a foundational concept for understanding our own significance and purpose. Knowing we are made in God's image helps us to understand the basis for the dignity and purpose of our life and work. Our worth and dignity are connected to our Creator. If God is of great and inestimable worth, then human beings made in his image must have great value, too.

My humble upbringing included emotional, physical, and psychological traumas, and as a result, it has taken me years to understand my value and gain a strong sense of love and belonging. It became clearer after I became a Christian that my worthiness comes from above. That is not always how the world views us, but it's how God sees His children.

As I continue life's journey, I find great fulfillment in showing my own vulnerability by stripping off the masks I wear to protect my heart. Oftentimes, I feel alone, but we have more commonality than we think with others, and we are connected despite our imperfections. As I tell my story and others bear witness or can at least relate to it, together we experience an overlapping consciousness.

We may think we want money, power, fame, beauty, eternal youth, or a new car, but at the root of most of these desires is a need to belong, to be accepted, to connect with others, and to be loved.

> *Like Christ, we must become bread for the world*

Where we came from or from whom we were born does not decide our legacy or our destiny. To survive in our lives, we must refuse negativity, whether in the form of thoughts, words, people, things, opinions, or life circumstances.

Had I not developed the power of thinking positively early in life, I would not be the person I am today. It was a long process but thankfully, over time and after many mistakes, I finally realized my unwanted thoughts undermined my self-esteem, which in turn, caused me to be vulnerable and insecure. For me to be happy and content with myself and my circumstances, I mastered how to immediately replace or reframe those negative thoughts.

The bible is filled with countless stories of people of faith who trusted in God with every aspect of their life. Such faith has allowed many people to persevere through hard times and to stay optimistic about the future.

At an early age, I knew my purpose was to impact peoples' lives through storytelling and writing. As you can read in my memoir, *Survive and Thrive Against the Odds,* my struggles began before birth. My dad was 73 and my mother was 49 when I was conceived; doctors recommended they terminate the pregnancy because I might have severe birth defects, perhaps including Down Syndrome. My parents agreed, however, on the morning of the abortion, my brother, Ray, hitchhiked two hours to the hospital to stop the procedure. Although my mother was already prepped and heavily medicated when my brother frantically ran into pre-op, she listened to him as he begged her not to have the surgery because of the hopeful dream he'd had the night before.

Then, as a toddler, I was severely burned. I was trying to pull myself up to walk and startled my sister Verna when I grabbed her legs as she was stirring the boiling contents of a large cast-iron pot. She jumped backward, and the pot and its contents landed all over me. Everyone was in shock and afraid to move me because of my raw, tender, burned skin, so I sat in the burning puddle until someone was finally brave enough to rescue me.

The doctors wrote me off for the second time with another inaccurate prediction: They told my parents I would never have normal skin and hair due to the severity of the third-degree burns. Thankfully they were wrong on both counts.

## Country Living

When I was about four years of age, I remember the loneliness when my sisters left for Texas to join our brother. Our wooden frame house seemed so desolate, but my chores increased drastically. My childhood consisted of endless farm work and household chores. My elderly parents' livelihood came mainly from farming, and they each lived on their own farm.

I didn't play with dolls and have playmates as other young girls my age did. My mother and I lived in a poor, rural area, and my time was spent planting vegetable and fruit seeds, watering the seeds, chopping weeds, harvesting the produce, and prepping it for sale. When it was too dark to see, sometimes I missed chopping the weeds and instead chopped my foot. I was tiny and short, and struggled with the tall gardening tools. When I made a mistake, my punishment depended upon my mother's mood and the degree of damage I had done to the plants. I lived in fear because I never knew what to expect.

As a four-year-old, I didn't see the plants as nourishment or income for our family but rather as torture and hard work. I learned to use my imaginative and creative mind to cope with the boredom and struggle. I didn't have playmates, but I had the animals and my superhero, God. I talked to God as if He were Superman. I told Him exactly how I felt about things I didn't like, as well as the dreams I had for my future. That was my way of doing what the preacher suggested when he told us to pray.

I told God all about country living and that one day, I wouldn't have to live that way. I also told Him I wanted a beautiful home, a modern car, and *no* antiques. Everything we had was an antique, not valuable old items but unmatched, worn-out discards. I went with my mother sometimes when she ironed for rich and middle-class people, and I saw the difference in their homes. I daydreamed and imagined that I was going to be rich, beautiful, and respected one day. Research shows that daydreaming helps us to get out of our limited perspective and explore other ways of thinking, which can be an important asset to creative work.

I'm still not sure if I was truly afraid of my mother, but I know I always made a concerted effort to please her. I learned early on that life was a lot better when she was happy. She passionately believed work was good for an individual and it didn't matter about age, size, disability, or whatever. If she worked, you worked, and you'd better act as if you enjoyed it.

When I was very young, we didn't have running water, so I had to draw water from a well some distance from our house. By the time I made it to the kitchen, the bucket would be almost empty, and I would start the process all over again.

We had to heat water for our baths and the laundry, which was my job to fold. I also fed the chickens, hogs, and cows, helped to make lye soap, and did everything else I was ordered to do. Being "too young" was not an acceptable excuse. I sure was a happy child when we finally got a pump for the well, and I was even happier when we moved out of the country to the edge of a town in northern Louisiana.

My dad's homestead was about 25 miles from my mother's home. He visited us faithfully every Wednesday evening at 6 p.m. I looked forward to seeing Dad's shiny black sedan come down the winding road as I watched from our screened veranda.

Dad owned and managed a country store along with some farmland. Each time he visited us, he brought me large cookies with our last name on them. Unlike my mother, who seldom showed me signs of love and acceptance, he was affectionate, and he picked me up, hugged, and kissed me while telling me he loved me. His warmth and love made me feel so special.

On one of his visits, he asked my mother if he could take me back to his home for a visit. Thankfully, she gave her approval. She packed the homemade dresses she had made for me and put together some cooked food for our lunches and dinners.

The next morning, we left for my father's home. As we got closer, he asked me to close my eyes. Once he gave me permission to open them, I saw the most beautiful Shetland pony grazing in his pasture. He had known I had wanted one for quite some time. When we got out of the car and put our things away, he saddled her up and placed me on it as he walked by my side. I was ecstatic.

Each of those few days with my dad was exciting and fun. He was old but acted much younger. When we got up in the morning, he prepared our breakfast. Then we went to his store. The customers were amazed my dad had a young daughter at his age and many believed I was his granddaughter. At the store, he taught me how to count money. The customers were very patient.

Because my dad's behavior was loving eventempered, I didn't have the nervousness I had around my mother. If I made a mistake, he didn't yell, curse, or beat me. Instead, he talked to me gently and taught me how to make the mistake right. Those few days with him taught me the keys of good parenthood, which I used years later when my own children arrived. My visit with Dad changed my life.

But all too soon, I had to go back home to my mother.

## Nothing Lasts Forever

Life taught me early on that change is always going to come. The next Wednesday evening, my dad did not show up as usual. I waited a long time and looked out of the window until late into the night. I even got up during the night to peep out of the cloudy, dusty window. The next morning my mother and I drove to his farm to check on him. When we finally made it there, my mother commanded me to stay put until she returned to get me.

She reappeared with sadness, and I knew immediately that he was sick or dead. Dad was lying on his back porch, covered with flies. I tried to shake him awake, but I knew he was gone. I was just five years old. My life with my mother moved on.

During my fifth-grade year, public schools in my small hometown finally were integrated, and I was one of the first black students to be bused to the white public school. Throughout kindergarten and elementary school, I had made all A's and B's, but in my new school, I had a rude awakening. I struggled and ended up failing fifth grade.

However, the Lord had a ram in the bush—my sister, Verna, who was a teacher. She moved back home because of some horrific circumstances she encountered in Chicago. Verna saved my life in priceless ways as an educator and Christian. Repeating fifth grade was easy for me after studying the entire summer. From that point on, I was an honor student. My name was in our small hometown newspaper every month, and my mother and sister eagerly showed the section to their friends.

Growing up and maturing was an interesting process. I battled mentally and emotionally with self-esteem and belonging. I was still a cheerleader when I became pregnant at 17 by my first-ever boyfriend. Alvin and I married and had a beautiful baby girl, and I graduated from high school as a happily married honor student and mother. I started college but dropped out because we relocated to Texas. There, I had two more children but continued to go to community colleges on a part-time basis for ten years while working.

Years later, after we moved to Texas, Alvin was killed in an accident. After his death, I chose to move on, and I finished my undergraduate degree and moved to Tennessee with a new husband. My new marriage was not good.

That's when my health started taking a turn for the worse. The stress of the bad marriage, my job, my husband's unemployment, and his failure to pay child support for his children created a lot of stress for me and my children. I experienced uncontrollable crying, hair and weight loss, skin discoloration, a rapid heart rate, and decreased concentration. My doctor ordered several tests, and I was diagnosed with hyperthyroidism. The next day I was scheduled to get the iodine radiation treatment.

During the next 60 days, I experienced even more emotional and physical turbulence. I was rushed to the hospital with breathing problems and then transferred to a larger and better-equipped hospital, where I was diagnosed with congestive heart failure, an enlarged heart, and leaking valves. During my health battles, I fervently prayed. My children had lost their father and I did not want to imagine them being without their mother as well.

It's interesting that we Christians want to go to heaven, but many don't want to die to get there, including me! I prayed and strongly believed Jehovah Rapha (*God Who Heals*) was more than able to heal me. One morning after my sister from Texas and my husband had visited me, I started to die. The nurses rushed in and moved me to the Intensive Care Unit where they attempted to resuscitate me, but I didn't respond. When my ex-husband and sister made it back to my home, they found a message describing what had happened to me, I was gone.

## It's Not Over Yet

Thankfully, there was another miracle. Although I had been pronounced dead when the medical staff pulled the cover off my face, they discovered my eyes were open and I was alive. I was hurried back into ICU.

After a few hours of recovery, I was moved back into my original hospital room, and family members from around the country gathered outside my room.

They weren't allowed inside so I was alone in the room when a stranger visited me. As he entered the room, chills ran all over my thin, frail 80-pound body. What's interesting is no one saw him come into my room and no one saw him leave. He approached the hospital bed, slowly reached out for my left hand, and began speaking calmly. He told me three things that made a powerful, positive impact on my life:

It was not my time yet, but the forces of evil were still trying to end my life early.

I had work to do that would positively affect millions of peoples' lives.

I should rest and know I would never be alone because I had divine protectors.

As he spoke, he squeezed my left hand tightly but gently. I wept. From that point on, I knew I had to write my first book, *Survive and Thrive against the Odds*, and share my story; I am a vessel to glorify God and His children, offering hope to the hopeless and faith to the faithless.

Although my family had some dysfunctional behaviors, I deliberately made a choice to recognize their gifts and values rather than focusing my energy on the baggage and negativity.

I knew early on I wanted to make something out of my life. When my mindset improved, I was blessedly able to see things from a different perspective. For instance, my parents gave me priceless lessons on work ethics, land ownership, entrepreneurship, mountain-moving faith, money management, and perseverance, all of which helped me throughout life.

I continuously try to examine my attitude, mindset, and choices, and what I have discovered is that making the right choices and having the right mindset decide one's spiritual, financial, educational, social, physical, and mental well-being, and also whether our lives go smoothly or become difficult.

Maya Angelou says this more gracefully than I can: *My mission in life is not merely to survive, but to thrive; and to do so with some passion, some compassion, some humor, and some style.*

It is an honor to be one of God's chosen vessels. As God's children, we must believe our lives are broken so they can be given to others. Like Christ, we must become bread for the world. When we live our brokenness under His blessing, our lives will continue to bear fruit from generation to generation.

My prayer is that my blessings come as a by-product of being useful to my fellow man.

# Author's Notes

My humble beginnings were in a rural, northern Louisiana community.

My family encouraged me to be obedient to God's word and stay focused. I paid heed to their advice and earned a Bachelor of Science from Grambling State University and a Master of Science in Organization Development from American University. I spend my life teaching, writing, and mentoring others in Jesus Christ, and have published a memoir, *Survive and Thrive Against the Odds*.

My daughter Niya is a wife, teacher, and poet. My daughter Narika is a wife, mother of two (Amelia and Josiah), a speech pathologist, and a teacher of the gospel. My son Namayo is a husband, father of two (Alvin and Averie), a teacher, and a minister of the gospel. Each of their spouses, Ron, Joshua, and Patrice are God-fearing and lovers of God.

## Contact Information

**Email:** Shirley.shirlaninc@gmail.com
**Website:** getsurvivetheodds.com
**Instagram:** shirley.lancaster.52
**Twitter:** @shirlaninc

Chapter 19

# Rising From the Ashes

### Carolyn M. Johnson

"**W**hy don't you just go out and get a job!" I can laugh at those words now, but I said them pretty loudly and snidely when my cousin, Bob Schmidt, first invited me to join him in network marketing. I was in my 20s and just launching a career in real estate. My life had been tough up to that point and I knew nothing came easily, especially money.

In my youthful and too-certain opinion, success and wealth were the results of having a really good job—or better yet, owning a brick-and-mortar business. Whatever Bob was pitching, I wasn't going to have any part of it. I rather rudely declined his offer and put it out of my mind.

It's funny how life changes. As it evolves, you shift the way you see the world.

A couple of decades passed, and cousin Bob reappeared. He was looking healthy, happy, and exceptionally well-to-do. He'd been living an extravagant lifestyle, the fruit of his smart labor and the testament to his immense professional success. There I was, still in the same town, still grinding away hour after hour. To be sure, I had enjoyed a certain level of success and achieved goals I'd set out to accomplish. I'd climbed the corporate ladder and even owned my own small business.

However, at that moment I was also drowning under a burdensome debt after the failure of a big stadium event I'd created and produced. Twice divorced, I was upside down, had sold my home, liquidated my assets, and was renting a ten-by-twelve-foot bedroom from a friend as I repaid enormous debts for which I'd assumed full responsibility.

> *If you are ready to move forward in your life, I offer my hand to help you up.*

It was all too apparent that my decades of diligent efforts, ambitious aspirations in the corporate world, and my own business had never given me any true financial freedom—and especially not freedom of my time. On the other hand, Bob was enjoying both; he had far more time and money than rightly seemed fair. He patiently encouraged me to take another look at network marketing. I finally realized I could trust Bob's leadership, and that time I did. I was ready to rise from the ashes.

When I remember the tiny rented room where I launched my new business, with space just for a bed, a dresser, and a computer table in the corner, I'm humbled and amazed at how far I've come.

Bob was serious about business, and I earnestly followed his guidance. I put his system in place, immediately began to make money, and began to retire my debt, a healthy chunk at a time. With Bob's direction, I laid out a clear business plan, and every single day, week after week, I progressed.

Within three years, my network marketing business efforts were more than amply rewarded. I was earning a *seven-figure* income—more money than I'd made *in total* during the first 14 years of my corporate career—and I did it from home with no employees and no inventory. I repaid my debts in a third of the scheduled time, and I bought a million-dollar home.

For many, it's hard to believe that you can start with no promises, no salary, no insurance, and no paid vacations—and end up creating a success rarely achieved as either an employee or a small business owner. *Seven* figures. *Three* years. Stunning.

Does that happen to everyone? Of course not. But my "why" was great, and I was serious and dedicated. I had good reason to rise from the ashes again. I knew the worst and wasn't about to relive it.

As a young girl, I grew up in the scathing heat of my father's perpetual anger and disappointment in life, and most directly with me. He wasn't a gentle person to begin with; he was prone to drinking way too much, and he had wanted a boy. He'd had three girls and I was the one he said should have been a boy... that my bedroom should have resembled my boy cousins' room . . . bats, balls, and gloves. It was hurtful and confusing when I was very small; my very presence seemed to make him angry and I could never please him. His scorn and cruelty drove me to search out others whom I could please instead: others' parents, priests, nuns, and most particularly, Jesus Christ himself. In my young mind, I thought if I could just make everyone happy, they—*and my father!*—wouldn't be filled with anger all the time.

I did continue to try to keep my father from becoming angry, though. God had given me a powerful will, but no amount of effort worked with my father, not kind words, being good, laughter, or hard work—none of it. Certainly, there were occasional happy moments in my childhood, like anybody else's, but the fear of being attacked emotionally and verbally constantly hunted me.

Abuse and alcoholism had run rampant through generations of my family, along with a patriarchal view of women and their place. College was for men; making babies was for women. Women shouldn't aspire to do the things men did. Being brought up to believe I was a constant disappointment to my father and family gave me a rampaging case of low self-esteem. The insults lived forever in my brain: *You're not pretty! You're not smart enough to do that! You will never amount to anything!*

I worked hard from the age of 14, keeping my head down, trying to please people, and do a good job. As soon as I graduated from high school, my world was upended when my mother escaped from her unhealthy marriage with my little sister in tow—leaving me behind.

At that time, I gave up. I was exhausted and I stopped trying to please everyone—even God, even myself—mostly my father.

As I looked at my prospects, and my father's expectations, college was never an option. I was supposed to get married and have babies—plain and simple. I did, however, make my father happy when I married an alcoholic just like him, an abusive 31-year-old, a chip off the old block. At 19, it was the only way I imagined I could both escape and please my father, and it was a classic case of jumping out of the frying pan into the fire.

My first marriage was turbulent in such a painful way that I search for words to describe it. Looking back, it's obvious it was a foregone conclusion that I would find myself tangled in cruel abuse again. It was something I had grown accustomed to from an early age, and although often terrifying, it was somehow perfectly normal. In my marriage, though, there wasn't just verbal abuse; my husband physically intimidated and hurt me as well.

After I had my beautiful baby girl, Cathryn, I escaped because I was not going to allow her to live a childhood filled with fear and lack of self-worth, as I had. When Cathy was almost five years old, I reunited with my high school sweetheart. We moved to Phoenix, Arizona, to be married and started over. Yes, I tried to go back to the good old days. The problem was, there weren't any good old days in my past.

While I managed to change my surroundings and my companion, I had brought *myself* with me, which included my view of the world and my place in it. My life couldn't completely change until I changed my views. What went on inside my head is as important as whatever happened on the outside.

My second marriage also had no chance of survival, and we divorced for the same reasons we broke up years before in high school: two different people, two different priorities, and the inability to communicate. Fortunately, something good came from our marriage, a handsome baby boy, Thomas. I'm blessed to work alongside Tommy in business today.

It was rather fortuitous that I found myself in Phoenix for my first and second acts of rising from the ashes. When I think of the symbolism of the *phoenix*, a universal symbol of rebirth and renewal, that fabled bird rising from the ashes, I realize God might have been up to something.

My life and struggles—a story of fall and recovery—are not uncommon to many women. I know now that no matter where we've come from, or what has passed in our lives, none of it matters. What matters is *what we choose to do now*. Today deals us a new hand, no matter which cards we were dealt before.

The gains in my life took hard effort, a willingness to leave the past behind, and a commitment to rejuvenate my soul with the goodness in the world.

When I realized I was the one who'd be solely responsible for myself and my daughter, my real business journey began. I convinced a dentist to train me to be a dental assistant in return for working for him for free and worked another full-time job to support us. The dentist secured a paying job for me with another dentist, but it would be two years before I had a full day off.

My knowledge of dental tools and how the products worked was rewarded when I was hired as the first female dental manufacturers' representative in the United States. I traveled across the country to work with other dental representatives (at that time all male), demonstrating our products on the dentists' patients, a sales technique not available to my male colleagues. I was not happy that the male sales reps made at least *six* times my salary, but my boss told me to be grateful for what I was earning because I was making top secretarial wages. Seriously? Equal pay for equal work was not even a glimmer in executives' eyes at that point.

Though I never reached wage parity, the owner of the business, George Seymour, became the first real mentor I ever had in my life. He taught me to travel on my own and made sure I was educated to succeed in a field that was considered men's business. I admit I was thrilled with the experience I gained and some of the perks of a salesperson's job—the travel, the chance adventure—even though I was still having to take extra part-time work to survive. My life had taken a corporate turn and I found it very different from the dysfunctional life I'd grown up in. I was eager, ambitious, and I knew I wanted to do something important with my life. I began learning about the world, other people, and myself.

When I joined Yellow Pages, my knowledge and my confidence grew exponentially as I learned marketing, advertising, public and community relations, and speaking, adding to my innate and learned sales skills. I was fortunate to have a manager early on that encouraged and supported my ideas and projects that were out of the norm for the longtime ways of doing business. That is when I began a lifetime commitment to self-improvement and personal development.

I started giving back to my community in many ways, including fundraising for charities and putting on community events. While sitting on a board for a home for battered and abused women and children, I did capital fundraising for a beautiful facility specially designed for children. When I became president of the Phoenix Ad Council, I became even more involved in causes and opened my world wider.

The telephone industry began its death spiral in the last few years of the twentieth century, and I left Yellow Pages to start a company with a partner. We went into cause-related marketing, publishing children's books that were sponsored by corporations, with a percentage of the profits going to children's hospitals. After we parted ways, I worked as a marketing consultant for small businesses, but found most clients didn't have the money to pay me; instead, they wanted to give me a percentage of ownership, which doesn't pay many bills. I'd been broke and underpaid before and wasn't about to regress.

With a new partner, I organized events and found immediate success; we were fearless and inventive, putting on huge rallies and events with marginal resources.

After a couple of years of booming business, I had the courage and resources—I thought—to launch an event of my own. I'd recently dedicated my life to

Jesus Christ, and I felt called to create an event with a Christian focus. *Light in the Desert* was the name of my super-event, and I spent a year working with friends, family, and other believers to bring this dream to fruition. I rented the Peoria Sports Complex, which has a capacity of more than 12,000 people. I cashed in my 401k, stretched my cards to their max, and on April 24, 2000, the crowds finally came to share in my dream.

Just not enough of them.

My life crashed and burned again, and it took a while before I arose from the ashes this time. I was determined to repay every penny. I worked out a repayment plan with my creditors, liquidated my assets, and moved into a small, rented room at a friend's house.

This is the moment I reunited with cousin Bob and the next dramatic turn in my life took place. I rose from the ashes yet again.

I realized I'd made a mistake with my first rude judgment about network marketing. When I hear the occasional scornful comments about our industry, I think back to those days when I told Bob to "go get a job," and I laugh; people just don't know what they don't know. The truth is, network marketing has been a reliable and productive way to make money since the 1700s—long before retail stores even existed. While our industry has had its share of characters trying to turn a quick buck, they're in *every* industry, not just network marketing.

Once again, I was blessed to have a mentor. Bob showed me the limitless possibilities available when we finally learn to step out of our comfort zones and believe in ourselves.

Network marketing is more than a career; it has given me extraordinary experiences, expanded my knowledge of the world, enriched my life with precious friends, and transformed both my self-worth and my net worth. These experiences and assets are not derivatives of products but rather sourced from the many kind, generous, and genuine people who held out their hands to help me up. That changed everything.

Because my passion is to coach and mentor women who, like me, have experienced abuse in their lives and are less than confident about who they are and what they can accomplish, I designed and launched *Women Building Bridges,* a program to teach women they are created for greatness and can accomplish their dreams. Four business partners and I traveled internationally to coach, mentor, and lift women, both personally and in business.

I tell them and tell you: Wherever you live on this planet, you, too, can rise from the ashes like a *phoenix* and transform *your* whole world. I have seen it. I have done it. I am living it.

If you are ready to move forward in your life, I offer my hand to help you up. Reach for it!

*Dare to dream. Create a plan. Find a mentor. Then* **do** *it.*

# Author's Notes

When I was 14, and working at the local five-and-dime, I never could have predicted my current life as an international entrepreneur, speaker, executive coach, and author.

In my 20s, I became the first female manufacturer's rep of dental products in the country—at one-sixth of my male colleague's wages—and had to work two jobs to feed and care for my daughter. I spent years in the corporate arena at US West Direct, starting in sales and moving up to executive positions.

Finally, I decided it was past time to become my own boss, and I founded an event-planning business with a partner. A highlight was creating, developing, and running Arizona Bike week, which included 11 major events and 128 vendors over nine days with more than 200,000 motorcycle enthusiasts in attendance. It's still a Phoenix-area highlight.

I also owned Cause & Effect, LLC, which supplied employee evaluation and training, business plans, marketing strategies, and financial forecast development to startups and small companies.

Because I knew the needs of abused women and their families, I created fund-raising programs to help and shelter abused women.

Since joining the network marketing industry 18 years ago, I've built an organization of 175,000 people in 42 countries. I founded Women Building Bridges, an international organization that creates events for women to foster self-improvement and learn the fundamentals of owning their own business.

My community involvement includes serving on the boards of many organizations, including the Governor's Office for Children, Faith House, Family Christian Care, and the Hotel-Motel Association, plus serving as an arbitrator for the Better Business Bureau and as president of the Phoenix Advertising Club.

I am a member of the Multi-Million Dollar Club and recipient of the Phoenix 2018 Outstanding Leadership Award by the Global Women's Summit.

I co-authored *Mastering the Art of Success* with Les Brown and Jack Canfield, and *The Women's Millionaire Club* with Maureen G. Mulvaney.

Born in Southern California, I've been an Arizona resident most of my life. I cherish time spent with my family—daughter Cathy, and son Tommy; grandchildren: Preston, Christian, Gabriel, Nathaniel, Jerry, and Sierra; and great-grandchildren, Simon and Eliza.

## Contact information

| | |
|---|---|
| **Email:** | Carolyn@AnyOneCan.me |
| **Website:** | www.carolynmjohnson.com |
| **Facebook:** | carolyn.johnson.501 |
| **Instagram:** | carolynpersonal |
| **Linkedin:** | carolyn-johnson-global-entrepreneur-1b437b16/ |
| **Twitter:** | CarolynJohnson_ |

## Chapter 20

# Grow Continuously

**Les Brown**

There's a saying that goes, *If the shoe fits, wear it.* But my mother, Mamie Brown, lived by a different saying: *If the shoe don't fit, make it fit!*

I remember Mama bringing home hand-me-down clothes at Christmastime from the families she worked for. One Christmas, she brought home some nice size eight leather shoes from one of the families. When I tried on the shoes, I couldn't get my feet into them because they weren't big enough.

When I told Mama I couldn't fit into them, I figured that would be the end of it. However, Mama called my sister, Margaret Ann, and told her to run some warm water into the bathtub and bring her some Vaseline. My sister did as she was told. As the water was running, Mama began rubbing my feet with Vaseline, then she stuffed my feet into those too-small shoes!

She instructed me to get into the tub and walk around in the water. "And you better not splash any water on the floor while you walking, either!"

I didn't know what the point was, so after walking around in the tub for a little while, I called Mama to let her know that the shoes still didn't fit. But she answered back, "Walk until they do!" I walked backward and forward for what seemed like forever. And, much to my surprise, after so many laps in the tub, the water-soaked leather became a comfortable eight-and-a-half—just my size!

> *It doesn't really matter what happens to you. What matters is how you deal with it!*

If it had been up to me, I would have just given up on having those nice leather shoes, because they didn't fit me. I didn't know they could be *stretched* into a perfect fit.

This reminds me of how people treat their dreams and goals. Many people refuse to stretch themselves because they feel *they don't fit* the requirements or can't measure up to the demands of what it will take to get there. The truth of the matter is, if you don't try, you will never know what you can or cannot do.

No matter what you think you know, you don't know enough about yourself to even doubt your own abilities.

According to the laws of aerodynamics, a bumblebee isn't supposed to be able to fly because its puny little wings are not big enough to hold up its large body. It's a good thing for bumblebees that they never studied aerodynamics and don't know about their ill-designed bodies. Despite what science says, they continue to fly anyway!

Sometimes you need to be *intelligently ignorant.* When you're targeted to be the victim of policies, politics, religions, cultures, ad environments that are stacked against you—systems put into place and intentionally designed to destroy your sense of self—you must be like the bumblebee.

Just like my shoes, you must **grow continuously!** There will be times in our life when you feel that you can't overcome the odds. However, when you continue to work on yourself and develop mental resolve, increase your skills, and surround yourself with nourishing relationships, you will be able to defeat whatever obstacles life throws your way.

Walk those laps around the tub of life until the shoe fits! Don't allow your circumstances to define who you are; create the circumstances you want for yourself! Stretch yourself until you fit the occasion and meet the requirements.

### Standing in a wheelchair

I've listened to hundreds of thousands of motivational messages to expand my mind, to raise my own bar, to challenge myself to reach beyond my comfort zone. Why? Because I know *to have something you've never had before, you have to become someone you've never been before.*

There is no way to know when all of the motivation that I've filled myself up with will be put to the test of application. But trust me, those tests *always* come!

One day, my son, Patrick, was pushing me through the airport in a wheelchair. It was the first time that I'd been in public without being able to walk. As you can probably imagine, I was embarrassed. I hung my head down, hoping that people would not recognize me, but many did and greeted me warmly. I tried to hide my feelings, but their facial expressions were clear; they felt sorry for me and some wanted to ask what happened.

In the middle of my embarrassment, I paused to ask myself, *Why are you ashamed that the people you're going to speak to will know your condition?*

I realized that I needed to grow and stretch myself for this new challenge and I certainly rose to the occasion. Even though I spoke on stage from a wheelchair, I received a standing ovation from the audience. It really encouraged me to know that people did not judge me because of my condition. They were focused on my message, and although I could not physically stand up, I stood up through all of them when I received their ovation! My *hunger* stood up in me and in them.

You must realize things are going to happen to you in life—things you can't even begin to imagine. It doesn't matter what happens to you. What matters is how you deal with it! I no longer need a wheelchair to get around, but even if I did, I would not hang my head down. I will always hold my head up high!

I should never have cared about the stares of the people looking with their questioning expressions because I realize in that experience there was an opportunity for me to *grow continuously*. That is true for every experience, no matter how uncomfortable or humiliating.

*Do not ever again let people—whether they're for you or against you—determine your level of growth and greatness! It's up to you to **grow continuously** in every situation.*

### Either you expand or you're expendable

To build my speaking business, I made so many calls that at one time I had a callous on my ear (people thought it was a big mole). I made over 100 calls each day. I even made calls on the weekends, when businesses were closed, just in case somebody was working overtime. Lo and behold, one day someone answered the phone on Sunday afternoon, and I met my first corporate client.

I had a dream of doing corporate training. As I methodically went through my list of contacts, I dialed the number for Michigan Bell corporate offices, a huge phone company. Someone picked up and I greeted him, saying, "Hello! My name is Les Brown. Do you, or someone you know, need a speaker to come in and motivate the salespeople to increase their performance?"

Bewildered, the person on the other end of the line said, "Do you know this is Sunday afternoon?"

I responded with just as much confidence as he'd projected bewilderment. "Yes, I do!" And I thought to myself, *Whoever's in working on the weekend is the person I need to talk to!*

He told me to come in the next morning so we could speak face-to-face. And that's how I landed my first corporate contract! I trained employees from Michigan Bell, Illinois Bell, Sprint, and AT&T—all because I was willing to do the things that others won't do.

No matter what your passion is or your dream is, you will have to learn to master it. A recent book came out with the message, "Average is over!" The question is: One day, will you look back in regret or delight for how you handled your dreams?

Maybe it seems extreme, making 100 calls a day to the point of getting a calloused ear. And you know what? It *was* extreme. I missed out on time with friends and family. I missed out on rest. I missed out on recreation, but that's what it took for the reward that I enjoy today. I don't regret what I missed. I delight in what I've gained, and how I've impacted the lives of billions of people around the world.

Make no mistake about it. If you're not growing, you're shrinking! We live in an area that literally operates at lightning speed. If you aren't plugged in, you're left out. Now, more than ever, it's critical to constantly reach further and *grow continuously!*

Alvin Toffler, the author of *Future Shock,* made a profound statement: "The illiterate of the twenty-first century will not be those who cannot read and write, but those who cannot learn, unlearn and relearn." He was right. Change is constant, particularly in this era. Being flexible and willing to *grow continuously* are the new basic requirements for success.

Advances in technology allow businesses to move at the speed of light and the direction can change in a millisecond. As the great Robert Shuler said, "We're living in a time where you either expand or you are expendable." You must be nimble enough to ride the waves of change or you will crash and drown. Maybe if I were in that same position today, working to build my speaking business, I'd send out 100 texts a day or make 100 social media connections or set up 100 webinars!

You need to understand what it is going to take to win at what you're pursuing. You must continue to train and educate yourself to remain relevant. *You must grow continuously. You've got to be HUNGRY!*

### Sharpening your ax

Abraham Lincoln said, "If I had six hours to chop a tree down, I'd spend four sharpening my ax." The strongest tool *you* have is your mind. We must constantly sharpen and develop our minds. I agree with American's foremost business philosopher and writer, Peter Drucker, who said, "This is an era of accelerated change, overwhelming complexity, and tremendous competition, facing us all."

A huge proportion of America's jobs will be permanently eliminated in the next few years due to the rise of artificial intelligence (AI), technology, cheap labor abroad, and apps. This doesn't even count job losses that have happened due to the pandemic. This is a time in which job security no longer exists. This is a time when you must have the mindset of an entrepreneur, control your own personal economy, create your own jobs, and make your own impact! *We're coming to the end of work!*

According to the Department of Labor, *before* the COVID-19 pandemic, more than 20,000 people were losing their jobs each month. During the pandemic, a million people were losing their jobs each *week*. Many others had pay cuts or hours cut. Too many of these jobs will never return.

The days of the 40/40/40 plan have come to an end. Working 40 hours a week for 40 years to receive 40 percent of your income is no longer a realistic plan, and not even an option after the employment market imploded in 2020. This is the time to ask yourself, *What is my strategy for being here? What's my next move?*

Sadly, so many people focus on making a living instead of living their making. Studies show Monday mornings have a thirty percent increase in heart attacks. People wake up to the grim reality of spending another forty-plus hours at a dreaded job they despise, and they often die on the toilet. So, you have a choice: To reduce your risk of a heart attack, you can either stop going to the toilet on Monday mornings, or you can start living the life you desire to live!

You must *grow continuously*. Grow in terms of your talents and skills and every area of your life. Put yourself in a position to get out of that dead-end job! As Mamie Brown always said, "Used-to-bees don't make no honey!" Never mind who or what you used to be. **Who and what are you now?** This is the time that you must challenge yourself! This is the time to develop at least three core competencies—three things that you are skilled enough to do to get paid for them. Become the person who can earn a living doing what you love!

Jim Rohn, who helped millions of people improve their lives, once said, "Work harder on yourself than on your job."

In the middle of the 2008 economic recession, Warren Buffet was asked what the most important investment was that people should make. This is a man who has made billions of dollars in the stock market and real estate. He answered, "The most important investment you can make is in yourself.

Mr. Buffett was correct—*you* are your greatest asset.

As an asset, you must find ways to appreciate it. Sometimes it's still hard for me to believe that I earn more in one hour than most Americans will earn in an entire year. I don't share this to impress you, but to impress upon you that:

*We shouldn't work to get paid by the hour;*
*we should work to get paid*
*for the value we bring to the hour!*

I want you to understand the power of investing in yourself. Knowledge is the new currency. Investing in yourself will yield the most profitable ROI (return on investment). Most of us never use the power that we have because we live in a world where we're told more about our limitations than our potential. This is why we must take the time to invest in our minds. We must acquire the knowledge to expand our vision of ourselves.

We must "sharpen our ax," sharpen our thinking and sharpen our skills. We must *grow continuously.*

Don't ever let fear hold you hostage. Now, more than ever is the time to grow, learn, strengthen your mind and your skills, and choose your future.

# Author's Notes

I grew up with two mothers, the one who gave my twin brother and me life, and the one who gave us love, Mamie Brown. We grew up in poverty in Liberty, City, Florida, and people told me to give up my dreams—they said I was the dumb twin. I knew, however, that my dreams were possible and I refused to give up. I had a hunger to take care of my mother, and I wanted to make a difference in the world.

I started in radio, filling in for a DJ when he became inebriated and couldn't do the show, and then getting a radio show of my own. I became a community activist, a state legislator for three terms in Ohio, and then moved into training and motivational speaking, something I wanted to do my entire life. For more than 50 years I've been teaching people how to overcome their obstacles, become one with their gifts, and share those gifts with the world.

## Contact Information

    **Website:**   lesbrown.com
    **Facebook:**  The Les Brown
    **Instagram:** @The Les Brown

Made in the USA
Columbia, SC
13 July 2022